I0095428

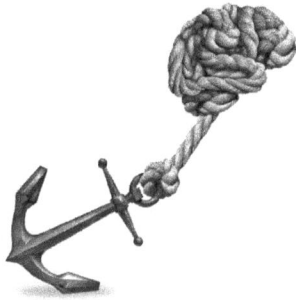

MIND KNOTS

UNDERSTANDING THE
COGNITIVE AND EMOTIONAL
BIASES THAT PREVENT
RATIONAL LEADERSHIP

LISA TROMBA

Cheval Press

COPYRIGHT © 2024 LISA TROMBA
All rights reserved.

MIND KNOTS
Understanding the Cognitive and Emotional
Biases That Prevent Rational Leadership
First Edition

ISBN   979-8-9890491-4-1 *Hardcover*
          979-8-9890491-5-8 *Paperback*
          979-8-9890491-6-5 *Ebook*

DEDICATION

To Michael and Cody:

As you practice every day to be the captain you aspire to be, remember...

Love and respect yourself and others. Let your ego guide a legacy of which you can be proud—one that elevates and enriches others.

Your knowledge is powerless unless you give it away so others can use it. Use your voice in your most effective way to make a difference.

When you think you're in control, remember it's just an illusion. Focus your energy on engaging, empowering, and inspiring others through the "power" of your ideas and messages.

Hold tight to your unique perspective against the gravity of conformity. But make sure your perspective is blended with the perspective of others—and firmly focused on the right outcome.

Let optimism fill your sails, but never ignore threatening winds and angry waves. Seeing reality and risk with clear eyes improves the vision, the journey, and the outcome.

Believe—but not blindly. Belief keeps you talking to yourself through waves of emotion limiting your perspective—creating your own false truth. Be skeptical—you might be wrong.

Consider potential destruction and regret left in the wake of acting on an unreasoned belief. Listen to others, seek honest evidence, and trust in what you learn, especially when the evidence disproves your belief. Blind belief never ends well. The integrity of belief matters.

Always listen to your inner voice: your intuition. And then listen to the logical voices of others.

Find the truth in your intuition through principled reasoning and data – the sound and savvy way.

Be cautious to not let your ideal plan hijack your execution. There is no perfect plan, no matter how long or hard you try to "boil the ocean" for answers. Aim to be imperfectly perfect: perfectly focused on your goal yet accepting the reality of imperfect timing, resources, and risk.

Finally, know your knots—the knots that tie you down, and the knots that can give you speed and move you forward.

Always in my heart,
Mom

CONTENTS

FOREWORD

by Dr. E. Ted Prince

It's funny how often in life and business things seem to work out for reasons we humans are blissfully unaware of. That's how my first meeting with Lisa Tromba went.

I had written a book on how leaders' financial styles impact their business and financial outcomes. I was running a seminar for consultants in the leadership space, and it just so happened that Lisa came along. I think we both recognized kindred spirits in each other, and we met later to compare notes. The common points were our interest in leadership. But the more nuanced discovery was that we both independently had come to the conclusion that leaders are all affected by unconscious drivers of which they are blissfully unaware.

My insights came from many years running companies as a working CEO. Lisa's came from rich experience in selecting leaders for a vast panoply of companies. Truth to tell, much of my experience came from my knowledge of myself. I was involved in selecting leaders but mainly from a board standpoint in other companies.

Lisa's experience comes from evaluating literally hundreds if not thousands of leadership candidates across a wide variety of industries. Her knowledge of those unconscious biases was formed as a result of assessing executives and then following the management and leadership performance of the executives she placed and presented to clients. She was intent on understanding cognitive biases because she understood that both a candidate's bias and a client's bias mattered for a successful and sustainable leadership solution. Not understanding them, or at least failing to be aware of them, is a disadvantage in these crucial decisions.

Some time ago, I wrote a book on these unconscious biases but mainly from a financial perspective. That was the basis for my professional work and the company I lead, Perth Leadership Institute. The work I was doing was based on the emerging discipline of behavioral finance. My work focused on financial styles and business personality—both reflective of cognitive biases. In my discussions with Lisa, who was well aware of this work, we remarked that leaders and indeed most executives, were either dimly or not aware of their existence.

When you get to the august position of CEO, or somewhere else in the rarefied height of the corporate environment, it's pretty rare that anyone ever has the courage or takes the opportunity to point out signals of bias. In fact, it might even be the opposite. So, how do you find out about these biases before your unknowing leaders are misled toward fatal mistakes or even total failure? After all, that happens to even the most celebrated CEOs and executives.

Both Lisa and I agreed that if you were to make any dent in this problem, you would have to get something to market to wise up bright executives who may not understand the reality that cognitive biases would sometimes lead them or the leaders they hire to fail. Worse still, at the point of failure they might still be blaming other people or external factors, rather than understanding that there were underlying forces at play of which they were unaware. And yet, the consequences of those underlying forces were theirs and theirs alone.

There is a pressing need to get the message out about these cognitive biases—to identify what they are; their impact on leaders, teams, and organizations; and actions one can take to moderate and control them. In principle, all easy to do, but in practice it is more difficult. That's because, as Lisa realized, there isn't much guidance on this specific to the leadership space. There were numerous publications that tied together personality and leadership, but they don't target this problem. In particular, there were no books on how to deal with these biases in a practical way.

There's a lot of cognitive biases: some books on behavioral economics and finance number them in the hundreds. But no one would read a book like that; it's just too much material. How would you filter those cognitive biases to the smaller number that would be comprehensive, practical, and useful to a working leader? And then how would you bring together solutions that hadn't been developed before?

There had to be a wealth of experience behind this endeavor since the people the book was written for were not neophytes but experienced leaders in their own right. If it wasn't to the point, pithy, and immediately useful, it would not get the job done.

That was where Lisa's depth of experience in executive search paid off. In executive selection, you've got to find leaders who are set to launch immediately. Those who recruit leaders must go well beyond educational qualifications, market familiarity, and professional experience.

They must get under the surface to figure out what is going on psychologically and how a leader's mind maps to the reality of the situation. Lisa's question became, "What cognitive and emotional biases could derail an otherwise brilliant executive, and are there ways I can prepare them with knowledge, which is apposite, empathetic, and accurate?"

That's what Lisa has done in this book. The unconscious biases I've been referencing are what she calls "mind knots." There are eight primary biases she covers, so the list is mercifully short and digestible—although she introduces more than forty mind knots showing the interplay of other related biases to the eight highlighted in the chapters ahead.

Since knots can often be a devil to unpick, she has developed an approach that breaks them down into a form a busy executive can use. Specifically, she shows the biases that can make a prominent bias worse, biases that can mitigate the problem, and countervailing biases, the attributes of which you can adopt to get you back to the points you need to occupy mentally in order to make a good fist of that new role. The approach is called the Captain's Compass, in keeping with the nautical leitmotif of the book.

"Knots" are a big deal if you're into ships and boats. They are part of a ship's captains' knowledge-set. CEOs and top executives are really captains in all senses of the word. Lisa's book leverages that concept to show how leaders can use that analogy to harness their own purposes in leading their own particular ship with its crew and contents.

All humans have cognitive biases—hard-to-unravel mind knots. These mind knots are part of the package when you hire a leader. We all have them, and all leaders have them. You need to figure out what your own prominent mind knots are and then what to do about them, preferably well before they have led to you getting shipwrecked. And if that happens, at least prepare the lifeboats, and figure out how you don't get marooned and back on board again.

Mind Knots is designed to be a handbook that aims to increase awareness of this important leadership dimension. Rather than being a theoretical tome, it offers clear guidance and practical actions leaders can take.

The idea is that leaders and aspiring leaders can get a fast take on the mind knots that can get in their way, and learn to manage them by understanding not only how to avoid making things worse, but even how to make those biases work for them.

Lisa's deep professional experience, coupled with the rich insights in this book, will be invaluable to aspiring and new leaders, as well as highly experienced corporate and entrepreneurial leaders who may recognize cognitive and emotional biases both in themselves and in others within their organizations. Importantly, these insights should make you stop and think as you are hiring your next leader.

I am looking forward to watching all of these constituencies reap the value of what Lisa has created.

—DR. E. TED PRINCE
Founder and CEO of Perth Leadership Institute,
author of *The Three Financial Styles of Very Successful Leaders*
and *Business Personality and Leadership Success*

INTRODUCTION

Organizations have often been compared to oceangoing vessels. There's the ship itself—the incorporated body—carrying valuable cargo from one port to another, under the command of the captain and crew, with investors and other stakeholders deeply interested in the outcome of the voyage. A successful trip means profits for all. Delays, damage to the ship, or even the ship sinking can spell financial disaster. No ship owner or captain wants to repeat the performance of the *Titanic*, a state-of-the-art vessel which, due to a series of human errors, didn't even make it across the Atlantic on her maiden voyage.

Guiding a major vessel laden with cargo and passengers across the open ocean to safe harbor is a complex task. The ultimate responsibility for the success of the venture falls with the captain. He or she must be professionally qualified but must also possess certain traits and strategies that ensure the exercise of sound judgment. The captain—and by extension every member of the crew—must be clear-headed, objective, and able to confront challenges without their judgment being clouded by preconceptions or personal biases. Having a desire to succeed is important, but expecting success under every condition can be foolish and lead to disaster.

In the mind of every captain can be found "mind knots." These are just what they sound like: distortions and tangles in perception and thinking that produce poor decisions, leading to bad outcomes that could have been avoided. It's a uniquely human problem. No one is immune. We bring to each decision the complications of our own preconceptions and biases. Sometimes we get lucky, and our biases actually produce a good result. But that's not often the case in complex situations. In leadership, where good judgment and decision-making are paramount, it's dangerous to think of mind knots as an asset. Without knowing how to manage them, mostly they are not.

Mind Knots is for leaders, teams, and businesses. The content of these pages lives at the intersection of leadership, business, and psychology.

I wrote this book to raise awareness of the reality of psychological bias, highlighting its importance and relevance to leadership. This book is about revealing the mind knots and biases that can distort our thinking and lead to bad decisions and learning how to manage them.

Mind knots describe cognitive and emotional biases, of which psychologists, scientists, and economists have identified over two hundred distinct types. These knots can wreak havoc for leaders at any level of an organization.

Understanding cognitive biases unlocks a key leadership lens that can bring focus and foundational insights to inform leadership selection, and a leader's journey. On a subconscious level, mind knots influence instincts, behaviors, capabilities, acumen, performance drivers, and emotional intelligence. Ignoring their existence sets the course for big problems. Yet, the risk these cognitive and emotional biases pose goes largely unnoticed because this lens is not typically applied in a leadership assessment and selection process.

Whether assessing leaders for specific roles or understanding their potential for higher-level roles in the future, organizations place a lot of emphasis on *cognitive capabilities*, a foundational measure of leadership potential. It is just as critical to understand mind knots, which cause *cognitive limitations*, hijacking rational leadership. This requires awareness and management strategies at both the leadership and organizational level.

Leaders and their biases are a package deal. And cognitive biases cannot be eliminated, only managed. To ignore them is to turn a blind eye to one of the greatest risks in leadership.

Cognitive and emotional biases are in play every day, swaying the decisions we make and the actions we take. Unmanaged, problems occur and usually compound. Understanding how our biases can sway and deceive us gives us the opportunity to identify signals and pick up clues that suggest we may not be seeing or thinking as clearly as we think we are.

You own your mind knots. Either you lead them, or they *will* lead you.

WHAT'S AHEAD ON THIS JOURNEY

Mind Knots explores the reality and ramifications of cognitive and emotional biases that cause leaders to go adrift, highlighted by the decisions they make and the actions they take—impacting their leadership and outcomes.

Choosing which biases to include in the book was defined by the leadership problems I was hired to solve. When an executive search is commissioned to replace a leader, sometimes it's because the leader is moving up in or out of an organization, but mostly it's because of a leadership problem—something is just not working out. Often the root of the problem isn't or can't be named, yet the symptoms are clear, and well-articulated through examples of less-than-ideal decisions, actions, or emotions the leader has made or demonstrated.

The *symptoms* clients shared revealed *problem* themes tied to a shortlist of issues related to ego, control, overconfidence, and emotions, among others. You may not be surprised to learn neither the leader's experience level nor the industry, function, business structure, size, ownership, or any other external factor could lay full claim to the theme or the problem. The underlying problem was the leader's mental lens—their mind knots.

So, the eight biases that headline the chapters of this book represent the most commonly emerging themes in the recent years of my work. And in each chapter, I include typical colluding biases to those eight, illustrating the broader mosaic of biases that conspire to influence our mental lens in unique ways.

Each chapter illustrates the significance of a particular bias through the lens of a leader archetype in which the bias is typically prominent. The featured biases in the chapters ahead are not unique to the captains described in the chapters, though for the purposes of illustration, the intensity of the bias and its repercussions tend to be closely aligned with the captain type described.

The first part of each chapter is focused on the featured bias, including what it is and how it shows up. The influence of the bias is illustrated through a real-life story of a captain highlighting the bias-influenced missteps they encountered, as well as their unfortunate and sometimes fatal outcome.

Every chapter offers two approaches to managing biases. The first approach is a navigation tool for the leader—a Captain's Compass that illustrates and explains how the attributes of other biases can either magnify, mitigate, or counter the effects of the chapter bias. This intervention requires *agile thinking and course correcting*, which is generally of greater use at the individual level and in a specific situation. Let's think of this as short-term *tacking*. Managing biases through short-term "tacks" is one approach, though not generally long-lasting.

Second, the final section of each chapter outlines "the rational approach"—a counter-bias or paradoxical strategy to flip the strength of these biases from knots that tie leaders down to knots that give them speed and move them forward to optimal outcomes. The optimal approach is achieved through a paradoxical model—a yin and yang of sorts that combines attributes and behaviors associated with opposing biases, resulting in a 1+1=3 outcome. Since you can't beat mind knots, you join them, so to speak.

The rational solution is illustrated through real-world stories that demonstrate the power of the counter-bias strategy outlined in each chapter. These nonfiction accounts tell stories of captains who, *either naturally or intentionally*, leveraged their prominent bias, alongside traits associated with a countering bias, resulting in leadership and business success.

To address the larger and looming issue of organizational bias, each chapter includes a counter-bias intervention model and tactics to safeguard the organization from detrimental effects and consequences of pervasive biases. This paradoxical approach outlines a model and guidance for the organization that leverages agile methodologies and practices, promoting anti-bias practices including feedback, perspectives, collaboration, integration, process control, and other methods to counter insidious biases that can hinder or harm the organization. Why is this important? Because too often, as the leader goes, so goes the organization.

This book offers an easy-to-follow and practical path to embracing and leveraging cognitive biases to empower leadership. The mission of the book is to inspire learning about mind knots, how to recognize them, and most importantly, how to manage and leverage these cognitive biases to support the individual leader and the organization.

MY PERSPECTIVE AND JOURNEY

My experience working with leaders spans over 25 years as a partner in three global search firms. Then, in 2020 I co-founded Luisi Tromba Advisors, which evolved into my current firm, Lisa Tromba Associates – Executive Search. Leadership Intelligence Services is a firm I founded in 2010 that continues to support my clients and my search practice with leadership assessment capabilities. My foray into executive search began in a private equity environment, where I worked with multiple senior leaders in the firm and gained exposure to boards and leadership teams across a portfolio of fourteen companies at various stages of development. My interest in leadership began during my foundational business experience with IBM, where I was graced with multiple learning and growth roles along the company's high potential leadership journey track.

Over the course of my career, I've been blessed with the great fortune of working with leaders in companies at all stages of evolution from lower mid-market to multi-billion-dollar global enterprises, across industries, markets, and countries, recruiting leaders for different contexts, situations, missions, and roles. Yes, that's a lot of leaders, with a lot of different biases. Some of those biases served them well...and many did not.

My passion and life's work are helping organizations and leaders to realize their leadership and business vision through clear thinking, reasoning, and evidence-based decision-making. Leadership selection is a critical business decision. Mental shortcuts don't work. Not for the organization, nor for the leader. And yet, time and time again, mind knots get in the way of leadership selection, performance, and ultimately, organizational outcomes.

Writing *Mind Knots* has been a journey of four-plus years. While my book journey began in 2019, my curiosity and the energy behind the book have been swelling for most of my professional life as both an observer and an unknowing host to cognitive and emotional biases. At first, I couldn't explain, nor did I have the understanding or vocabulary to describe, the phenomenon of psychological biases. Intrinsically motivated from both a personal and professional perspective, I was committed to figuring it out, and to helping others to understand the phenomenon as well.

Heeding and leveraging the evolving wisdom of the pioneers and experts in behavioral economics and finance, my writing acknowledges the reality of "mixed rationality" in the leadership space, while highlighting a largely overlooked leadership lens: cognitive bias or, more plainly, *mind knots*.

Mind Knots was written to increase awareness of psychological biases, intending to wave the flag, inspire caution, and thoughtfully illustrate the importance and relevance of cognitive and emotional biases to the science of leadership. Why? Because these mind knots can and will undermine most conventional dimensions considered to be indicators of a leader's potential for success.

We can do a better job by paying attention to these unconscious forces that tangle judgment and decision-making, ultimately hijacking rational leadership. *Mind Knots* will help you understand many of these biases and will show you how to strategically harness them for stronger leadership and business outcomes.

GETTING THE MOST OUT OF THIS BOOK

Aim to Increase your Awareness

We are all hardwired with many psychological biases; the prominence of each varies from person to person. Knowing ourselves includes developing an awareness of the cognitive and emotional biases that are always at work below the surface in our subconscious.

Leaders who recognize their predispositions, and how and when to challenge them, can and will improve their judgment, reducing errors in the decisions they make and the actions they take.

Knowing how to use our mind to organize our thinking and to manage our emotions in ways that keep us out of trouble is only possible if we can recognize our unconscious tendencies.

Learn to Recognize your Biases

While it's not easy, when we can recognize our biases, we are better positioned to steer our minds to manage our thoughts and emotions in ways that will protect us, our teams, and our organizations. Then, we can adopt strategies to use our cognitive and emotional inclinations to work for instead of against us.

Decisions made under the influence of mind knots produce errors. You have two choices to address this: to correct the error produced by a poor decision after it has been made, or to adopt an intervention strategy before making a decision.

Mind Knots focuses on the latter option. Throughout the book, I've included incisive questions to instigate pause, reflection, and thinking, all useful in deflecting unconscious errors in judgment that cause missteps.

Practice Intervention Strategies

I'll launch you into this *Mind Knots* journey with a simple question to ask yourself as you read through the chapters, and then every day after you put down this book. Why every day? Because mind knots are at play every day. They're not just tempting you in times of big decisions. They can steer you at any moment before you know what is happening.

First, I'll share a quick story that highlights the importance of the question I'm about to ask you.

An individual whom I was coaching was among a large group of invited guests attending a talk given by the CEO of a Fortune 50 company. Toward the end of the CEO's talk, the individual spoke up inappropriately in reaction to a particular comment the CEO made. The room went silent. The CEO paused and responded to the challenge with grace and character, providing a valuable learning moment for everyone in the room, particularly for the individual who reacted instinctively. Following the meeting, the circling question was, "What was he thinking?" The answer is—*he wasn't*. The mind knots that roped him were overconfidence and ego. The consequence of his momentary mental kink demonstrated who he was practicing becoming, and his error shifted the course of his journey.

So, as you read through this book, and then every day after, ask yourself, and answer honestly—"Who am I *practicing* becoming?"

While the question is future-focused, its true answer is revealed in actual responses in present situations.

How can this question help defend us against our mind's missteps? Because it taps into our human instinct of self-consistency, urging us to behave in ways that validate our self-concept—present or future. The prospect of behaving in a way that is inconsistent with our self-vision creates cognitive dissonance, which makes us uncomfortable, motivating us to maintain consistency with our self-vision – and in the spirit of this book, to be a clear-eyed leader, as demonstrated by good judgment and thoughtful decision-making.

Asking ourselves the question every day can serve as an intervention and thinking tool that can steer how we approach and respond to situations—because it prompts us to *pause and think* ahead of our response, ideally thwarting an unmanaged reaction influenced by a mind knot.

Ready? All Aboard!

ONE

COGNITIVE BIASES, THE SELF, AND SWAY

OMEWHERE IN THE WORLD, AT THIS VERY MOMENT, in the executive suite or boardroom of a corporation or nonprofit, the organization's top leaders are assembled around the table. They have one burning question on their minds: "Where did we go wrong?"

They're not talking about a bad investment decision or a faltering product rollout. With the right application of teamwork and imagination, those things can be fixed.

No, they're concerned about a much more difficult and potentially expensive problem.

A problem with a top executive. Perhaps even with the CEO.

This person was hired with the best of intentions. Perhaps he or she came highly recommended or boasted an exceptional track record at some other organization. During the interviews, this person offered all the right responses, had the right executive presence, and connected well with stakeholders.

And yet, a few months, maybe a year later, the signs are unmistakable: This executive is not a good fit. He or she is creating negative effects that are compounding across the company.

The organization is losing money, time, and possibly talent, and this leader is a key part of the problem.

But separating this executive from the organization will be expensive, the leadership team says. We'll need to offer a severance package. We'll need to search for a successor. The process will take time and money.

Some leaders at the meeting will say there were red flags. Certain things about the new hire seemed "off." But at the end of the day, the person's assets seemed to outweigh their liabilities.

Or so they hoped.

Making hiring errors, especially at the executive level, is expensive. The wrong leader, especially in the C-suite, can drag down the other employees working alongside him or her. The wrong leader at any level can cost the organization directly in lost sales, lowered revenues, inefficiency, poor employee engagement, unhappy customers, and even public relations blunders.

The U.S. Department of Labor (DOL) estimates the average cost of a bad hiring decision is at least 30 percent of the individual's first year expected earnings. If you consider an executive with an annual salary of $300,000, an annual incentive bonus of 40 percent, and a signing bonus on top of that for a total cash package approaching $500,000, based on the DOL's estimation, the direct cost to the organization would therefore be nearly

$150,000. But most "real-world" experts argue the cost can be much greater—as much as five times the annual salary, or in this case, over a cool million dollars.

THE IMPORTANCE OF CLEAR THINKING

Having made the painful decision to cut ties with this person, the next question becomes, "How do we avoid making the same mistake again?"

People are arguably the most important part of your company. Every organization faces challenges, and you need the very best people and leaders to jump those hurdles and keep your business growing and profitable. A mismatched leader can cause the entire organization to stumble and fall.

There are many reasons why a leader will not be a good fit for a position.

Perhaps they lack the appropriate "mission" experience, and therefore they just don't align with the context of the business situation and goals. Or they don't quite have the proven experience required for the role, or they don't click with the leadership team.

But many candidates seem like a good fit because they say all the right things and have all the right answers, have relevant experience and a good track record with a prior company, along with strong interpersonal skills and executive presence. And yet, the match isn't perfect. Something is off, but you can't put your finger on it.

This is because we choose leaders in part because of what they've done in the past, but also because of what we think they can do *in the future*. We try to choose leaders who we believe can solve problems we see coming, as well as problems we may not even know about yet.

One of the most important personal qualities required by a leader is the ability to *see clearly*. By this I mean the ability to look at a problem objectively, without bias or preconception. If a leader can do this, they have a better chance of choosing the correct solution and not some random or familiar one that they're attached to for some personal reason, but which bears no relation to the problem.

We don't know what the problem is.

But we do know that unless you approach the problem with clear eyes, an open mind, and without preconceptions, you run the risk of seizing upon the wrong solution.

Your mind is the lens through which you view the world. It guides your thinking, decision-making, emotions, behaviors, and the consequences that follow.

A leader's mental lens matters.

THE OBSTACLE: COGNITIVE BIAS

You don't want to be the executive who approaches a problem with preconceptions, prejudices, or a cloudy mental lens.

Neither do you want to *hire* such a person—not for any position, and especially not for an executive, CEO, or board role.

However, everyone has preconceptions and a unique data repository in their subconscious which affects their mental calculus. We all have *cognitive biases*. The key is to understand what they are, how they show up, and how to manage them to work for instead of against us.

What's cognitive bias?

First identified by Amos Tversky and Daniel Kahneman in 1972, cognitive bias is the tendency of the human brain to simplify incoming information to make it easier to understand and act upon. Cognitive biases help us find mental shortcuts to assist in the navigation of daily life and work.

The process of simplification is performed by a filter composed of personal experience and past events. As information is received, it's processed by those personal filters, which can *alter the substance of the information itself.* The brain then embraces a reality that may be a distortion of what really happened and what other people see. If the information involves a problem to be solved, then the solution—based on faulty data—will be a failure.

You can think of cognitive biases as knots in our minds that constrain the serious work of thinking in favor of quickly tying a perceived situation to a simple response. Cognitive biases are *"mind knots."* They hitch us to mental habits triggered by familiar circumstances. And it's hard to change habits—as anyone who's tried to do so knows.

To be fair, in a case where a split-second decision is required, cognitive bias can be useful.

For example, let's say you're walking along a desert trail and suddenly you see what appears to be a rattlesnake in front of you. You instantly think, "Oh—rattlesnake! Poisonous! Dangerous! I'd better move away from it!"

Your cognitive bias has kicked in and simplified your response.

But wait a minute—isn't it possible that what you thought was a rattlesnake was in fact a harmless gopher snake? The two species are similar in appearance and often confused.

Sure, it's possible. But you didn't wait to find out. Thanks to your cognitive bias, you came to a quick conclusion. And it may have been the correct one. Perhaps it would not have been wise to inspect the snake to determine if it were a deadly rattlesnake or a harmless gopher snake—you may have gotten bitten.

We use our cognitive biases every day. When you see a car speeding toward you, you think, "That's a reckless driver—I'd better move!"

When you hear thunder, you think, "A storm's coming."

These are examples of cognitive biases at work in useful or harmless ways. But too often, cognitive biases can produce negative results.

CHANGE IS THE ENEMY OF COGNITIVE BIAS

Cognitive biases can produce significant negative effects in leadership and business.

Why in business in particular?

Because the business environment is *constantly changing.* Operating realities that may have been true or accepted as fact even a short time ago may today be false. The competitor whom you used to ignore may now be poised to overtake you. The laws governing employment and discrimination have evolved. Technology that was cutting-edge yesterday will be obsolete tomorrow. The marketing plan that worked well a decade ago is probably worthless now.

In short, the solutions that dependably worked yesterday may not work today. What were once simple mental shortcuts have become dangerous mental models and habits. But when circumstances change, these ingrained simplified mental habits become detrimental because they tie us in place.

Because every business challenge and every opportunity are likely to be fundamentally *new*, each must be approached objectively and thoughtfully—with unconstrained thinking.

MIND KNOTS

Cognitive biases cannot be removed, nor can they be easily untangled. That's why I call them *mind knots*. They tangle your thinking, judgment, and decision-making.

Mind knots are stubborn and prevail more times than not. When it comes to hiring an executive for a position of responsibility, having a glimpse into the primary mind knots to which they are predisposed can be game-changing. Why? Because managing a leader's mind knots inevitably becomes an organizational affair—one that can result in a positive outcome, or one that can go really badly.

Mind knots prevent rational leadership by causing flawed judgment, poor decisions, bad behaviors, and negative consequences for business outcomes.

Understanding mind knots informs how someone processes information, situations, experiences, and challenges. Mind knots affect the decisions they make and the actions they take. This can bring focus and foundational insights to our view of leadership capability, including strategic thinking and judgment, operating style and communication, instincts, competencies, acumen, values, performance drivers, and emotional intelligence.

Through the lens of leadership, we learn more about mind knots and the practical, pervasive effect they have on leaders, teams, organizations, and the business ecosystem.

Leaders—especially because they hire other leaders —need to understand the reality and ramifications of cognitive biases. But that's not enough. The goal is to go beyond creating awareness and offer strategies for managing these mind knots, as well as a framework to flip the strength of these biases from knots that tie leaders down, to knots that give them speed and move them forward to optimal outcomes.

THE SELF

Mind knots create a form of tunnel vision in which the leader—let's call him or her the captain, as in the captain of a ship—perceives everything through a personal lens. The self, consisting of all the beliefs, memories, and preconceptions held by the captain as a result of the mind knots that live in the captain's subconscious, becomes preeminent.

Let's say a ship is on a long voyage across a vast ocean. It has no GPS—the captain must navigate by dead reckoning. For a highly trained individual, this challenge is not so difficult. In ancient times, Polynesian navigators piloted their oceangoing canoes by using a navigation system based on keen observations of the stars, ocean swells, bird flight patterns, and other natural signs. Near the equator at night, the entire celestial sphere would be exposed. Each star had a specific path known to the ancient wayfinder, and when these stars rose or set, they gave a bearing for navigation. Likewise, the size and direction of waves and swells could signal the presence of islands and atolls by their effects on the ocean currents. Navigators living within a group of islands would observe and learn the effects various islands had on the shape, direction, and motion of the currents, allowing them to correct their sailing path in relation to the changes they observed. In such a system of keen observation, *there is no self*. Yes, of course there's a high level of practical training. These ancient mariners trained for years to learn the secrets of navigation, just like a doctor studies for years. But extensive training and mind knots are *two different things*. You can be ignorant—with little training—and have massive mind knots. On the other hand, you can have multiple degrees and years of industry experience and also have massive mind knots. In both cases, the self has become dominant. The self and its various needs and desires color your perceptions. Your cognitive biases dominate. You see what you want to see and make your decisions according to what aligns with your preconceptions.

If you were a Polynesian captain of an outrigger canoe and allowed your personal preconceptions to override what you actually observed in the sky and the waves, you'd end up in the middle of nowhere, far from the safety of an island.

SWAY

Mind knots bring the self to the forefront during critical decision-making events. Allowing the self to dominate means that new, objective information is likely to be either ignored or distorted.

This is a problem in any position on a ship. But let's be honest—it's a bigger problem at a leadership level. When the captain—the CEO or a key leader in the business—is unaware of the mind knots that cloud his or her judgment, you've got a significant problem.

A leader has *sway*. This means the leader has authority and influence over others. He or she can make billion-dollar decisions. They can hire and fire top executives and managers. How they lead sets the tone of the culture of the rest of the company.

For example, Steve Jobs had tremendous sway over Apple. He was an extraordinarily hands-on leader who did not hesitate to make his opinions known. And—amazingly—he showed little evidence of letting his mind knots get in his way. Rather, Jobs's intuition bias not only served him well from a visionary perspective but was the underpinning of organizational collaboration. Intuitively, through "unplanned interaction and collaboration," Jobs harnessed ideas from across the organization. By creating open spaces that drew employees together, Jobs "forced" spontaneous encounters which served as a source of collaboration, inspiration, culture-building, knowledge-sharing, and idea development. Under his leadership, Apple made the right choices and rose to dominate its industry and market. Jobs was more than willing to discontinue products and programs that were not profitable. He saw the path ahead clearly and directed the company accordingly.

Speaking of Apple in contrast, let's examine the case of John Sculley, who proved to be a clear example of a poor leadership hire. The name might not ring a bell, but in 1983, the board of Apple hired Sculley to serve as CEO. Because of his significant business experience and marketing acumen, including the top job at PepsiCo, the board hoped Sculley would be "the adult in the room" and channel Jobs's restless genius.

In 1985, Sculley abused his power and convinced the board to strip Jobs of all managerial responsibility, effectively firing one of the greatest product designers and marketers of all time. Unfortunately, Sculley's marketing skills did not compensate for his poor product management and judgment. Lacking sufficient technical background to be a product manager for Apple, during his tenure he invested heavily in several failed ventures, including Apple's Newton (an early PDA-like device), cameras, and CD players. In 1993, Apple's board fired him.

To be fair, Sculley had great success in many other ventures. His experience with Apple was a case of his skills and mental lens being a mismatch for what the company needed. In some cases, a leader's cognitive biases aren't relevant to the tasks at hand and cause no harm. But the combination of John Sculley and Apple was not a good match, and his cognitive biases resulted in some very bad decisions.

WHEN YOU HIRE A CAPTAIN

We all have mind knots—some small and inconsequential, some big and powerful. If you choose to embark on a program of self-awareness, self-analysis, and self-improvement with the goal of mitigating and managing your mind knots, the lessons of this book will prove invaluable.

In general, though, this book is designed to provide you with insights on how mind knots affect the thinking processes of leaders—captains of your ship, if you will—and how those thinking processes will impact their decision-making. Hiring and onboarding a new captain is always a stressful process but armed with the knowledge revealed in the following chapters, you'll be better able to determine which potential leader is best positioned to ride the waves of change for your ship.

MIND KNOTS NAVIGATION MAP

In the following chapters, we'll explore many variations of mind knots—what they are, how they can negatively impact leadership and business, and how to manage them. We will discuss eight mind knots in detail in Chapters 2 through 9, through the perspective of an archetypal "captain," such as the Captain of Self and Sway in Chapter 2. Each chapter includes examples of captains whose mind knots tied them down, as well as examples of captains whose knots gave them speed and moved them forward. The stories in each chapter are real, and so are the consequences, negative and positive, of each captain's mind knots.

The first part of the solution is gaining awareness of the bias, recognizing it, and managing it for good. Cognitive biases cannot be eliminated or erased from our subconsciouses. They can, however, be managed and tamed. Self-awareness opens the throttle for adjusting the course and steering toward an improved outcome.

Each chapter offers two types of guidance for managing the negative effects of the mind knot in your leadership.

The Captain's Compass provides navigational guidance in the form of *tacking* techniques for managing the bias at an individual level.

The Rational Solution provides guidance and guardrails for bias management at the organizational level to prevent a systemic wave of negative effects common to the bias. Because, as we know, "As the leader goes...so goes the organization."

TACKING WITH THE CAPTAIN'S COMPASS

Primary Bias

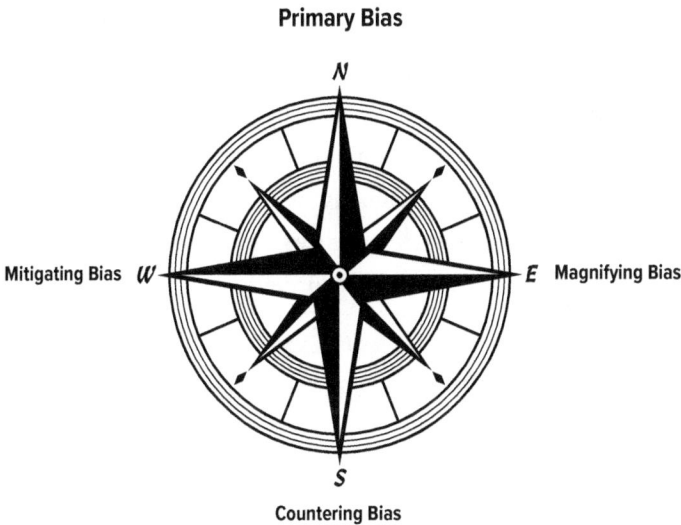

Mitigating Bias　*W* — — — *E*　Magnifying Bias

Countering Bias

On a ship, the Captain's bridge is the hub for judgment and decisions. It's where situations are assessed, approaches are considered, judgment is levied, and decisions are made. It's where complexity is processed, organized, and translated into strategies and action. It's where mental agility matters—and where the Captain's Compass can be an important thinking tool.

The Captain's Compass (Compass) is a navigation tool for captains affected by any of the biases featured in this book. Each chapter includes a Compass illustrating how certain mind knots can alter the captain's course. Through its cardinal points, the Compass illustrates potential routes for these captains—one to avoid that would make the journey even more perilous, and two possible routes to a safer course, improving the odds for a successful mission.

The Compass illustrates that by deliberately adopting attributes associated with other biases, the effects of the primary bias can be altered, either increasing or decreasing the leader's odds of success depending on choices they make and actions they take. Biases are directional—moving us toward or away from a tendency. The Captain's Compass is an intervention tool that considers the directional tendencies of other biases that will either help or hinder a captain's journey.

THE RATIONAL SOLUTION

The Captain's Compass provides effective short-term tacking strategies for the captain. While short-term tacks may be effective in keeping captains on a safer course, the real payoff is realized when a systemic plan for the organization is implemented and executed to guard against pervasive mind knots.

The final section of each chapter maps the course to a rational solution. The starting point is awareness both at the helm and throughout the realm.

In this section you'll find a story of a captain who, despite the prominence of the bias, was able to successfully manage it, and even leverage it for a positive outcome. This is the result of employing paradoxical thinking—sometimes intentionally and sometimes naturally.

The Rational Solution section of each chapter is focused on bias management and guidance at an organizational level. The guidance is broad and offers practical operating practices to reduce bias errors while creating a wave of engagement and bias management across the organization. Most importantly, the model presented in each chapter offers a counter-bias approach to leveraging biases to work for, instead of against you and your organization.

Every human being has cognitive biases. Some may be more prevalent than others. The goal is to recognize, minimize, and manage them, and ultimately to leverage them for positive leadership and business outcomes. As you will see in the chapters ahead, by employing agile and paradoxical thinking, you will find the route to a more rational solution.

THE EGOCENTRIC BIAS

THE FIELD OF BEHAVIORAL SCIENCE RECOGNIZES HUNdreds of cognitive biases. These biases—or mind knots—are hidden in our subconscious, wreaking havoc on our judgment and decision-making. Because of their subconscious nature, we are typically unaware of our mind knots ... until they get us into trouble.

And they usually do.

Egocentric Bias is no exception. And in the case of leadership, it can be a big problem.

This mind knot impels leaders to see and move in one direction: their own. Egocentric leaders focus on their own opinions, while blurring the perspectives of others. These leaders typically latch onto people and data that validate their beliefs, while avoiding dissenting information.

CAPTAINS OF SELF AND SWAY

Captains of Self and Sway typically operate in their own alternate reality, protecting their strong sense of self. They are obsessively bound to themselves, their beliefs, and their often imagined but unrealistic capabilities.

On the surface, Captains of Self and Sway offer a compelling leadership profile. These are often leaders with extraordinary vision and unrelenting ambition fueled by passion, unbending belief, and unwavering confidence. Goal-oriented and persistent, these captains operate with grit and gumption. They speak with conviction and act with intensity, positivity, and often boundless energy.

Captains of Self and Sway can be charismatic and inspirational, and their magnetism is typically rooted in emotion. Yet, these leaders are usually blind to the emotions of others, positioning them pretty low on an empathy scale. Due to their individualism, teamwork and collaboration are not their preferred way of working.

Transparency, trust, and even integrity can hang in the balance with captains whose egocentric bias is their beacon. Egocentric bias creates a false sense of self that operates in opposition to truth, and this mind knot can sink captains, crews, and entire ships.

Over time, due to an unmanaged egocentric bias, these leaders usually unravel teams and organizations, threatening missions and outcomes.

However, when egocentrism is managed, Captains of Self and Sway have the potential to:

- Inspire with intensity, confidently leading others toward their vision.
- Envision a winning strategy, sometimes creating new markets.
- Direct and drive the execution of their strategy.
- Achieve strong positioning for themselves and their organization.
- Leverage strategic alliances to advance their position.
- Attain power in pursuit of their purpose.

These individualists also use "personal presentation" to increase their power, and to advance their individual position, and sometimes their company's position as well.

FIRST IMPRESSIONS

Characteristics associated with egocentric leaders include drive, passion, optimism, confidence, and conviction—often among the characteristics sought by organizations for which leaders are selected.

Leaders who possess these attractive traits may appear at first glance to be promising captains, especially when their experience and accomplishments align well with the context, situation, and role for which they are being considered.

First impressions can be deceiving. Yet, characteristics such as those listed and others can sway a selection team to hire leaders with strong front stage skills to lead the mission.

But at what cost?

The critical question becomes: *whose* mission—the captain's or the company's?

What if these seemingly "winning" leadership characteristics are tainted by personal ambition and a deeply flawed belief?

What if the captain's mission is their alternate reality?

What if the mission is the captain's obsession?

And worse, what if the captain is their own obsession? And that is the problem organizations too often face.

Every one of us has an ego, and to some degree we are all affected by the egocentric bias. But does this threatening bias control us, or can we control it?

In this chapter, we'll explore the egocentric bias, a mind knot that binds Captains of Self and Sway to their self-centered filters, making them captains of "Me, Myself, and I."

The egocentric bias, contrary to its holder's *self-boosting* intent, is often *self-defeating*.

There are many "selves" associated with Captains of Self and Sway, including self-serving, self-aggrandizing, self-absorbed, self-enhancing, selfish...However, the most important self-focus, of which these captains typically have none, is self-awareness.

PASSION, EGO, AND CHARISMA

Captains of Self and Sway are often described as "passionate," making them stand out in most environments. The problem is passion isn't directly correlated to a good outcome. Why? Because passion is based on emotion.

Brad Stulberg and Steve Magness, authors of *The Passion Paradox*, point out, "All the greats shared something in common: An unrelenting drive. An eternal hunger. An inability to be satisfied. Passion."

I don't disagree. Most of us admire passionate people and the energy and positivity they exude, though passion can be misinterpreted and overrated. In combination with the egocentric bias, passion is an ominous and ineffective indicator of success. Let's face it: in the leadership arena, there are plenty of examples of leaders who possessed a passionate drive but never made it to the "Greats" list.

What you see is not always what you get. Misguided, misaligned, or even manufactured passion will inevitably steer these captains off course.

Egocentric leaders are often charismatic, creating a magical and almost magnetic aura to which others are attracted and pledge themselves emotionally. Feeling valued, important, and even revered elevates their sense of self-worth. Charisma compounds the directional risk of egocentric bias, attracting followers who are easily swayed by the leader's perceptions and beliefs, rather than their own.

In its extreme form, egocentric bias leads to a grandiose sense of self-importance. Affected Captains of Self and Sway can live in a world of fantasy that revolves around their need for notoriety. Hitched to an alternate reality driven by self-centered ambition, these captains can become masters of illusion.

Here is the story of one such captain.

Elizabeth Holmes: The Queen of Make-Believe

Elizabeth Holmes, founder and CEO of the now fallen Theranos, is an extreme version of the Captain of Self and Sway and a perfect example of the ill effects of the egocentric mind knot. Launching Theranos in 2003, she envisioned revolutionizing healthcare with a technology solution that would enable people to manage their health more conveniently and affordably. She claimed her portable "black box" or "mini-lab" could perform comprehensive blood screening in real time with one drop of blood from a simple finger pinprick.

Touting fiction and false promises, Holmes passionately and charismatically lured in followers by delivering her case through emotional appeal. Peering into her audiences, with her big, blue, unblinking eyes, she deceptively repeated her mantra, "No one would ever have to say goodbye too soon."

Maintaining her conviction and confidence, the only thing Holmes was sure of was the iconic status she'd achieve if she brought her imagined "scientific breakthrough" to fruition.

Despite her perfectly manufactured image, her self-awareness was little to none. Proving to have a significant empathy gap, she demonstrated a blatant disregard for others' perspectives, even as her ship was sinking.

She held sway over powerful, intelligent people.

Holmes intentionally surrounded herself with these highly acclaimed legends to bolster her credibility. She charmed them through passion and emotion, and they became her influencers and social proof.

Her cleverly constructed board in turn led her to well-pedigreed, non-healthcare investors for a combined capital raise of over $1 billion. Despite maintaining 90 percent control and stripping them of any real power, the compliant board members enabled her to operate in the absence of transparency. Why? Because they were tied to their belief in a positive outcome.

They were the holders of the Positive Outcome Bias, a mind knot that magnifies the effects of egocentrism by seductively tying others to a sexy, imagined outcome. While Holmes's egocentrism steadily steered Theranos into the storm, her believers in the positive picture she painted provided the wind in her sails.

Fortune magazine jumped on the bandwagon, producing a splashy piece with big blue-eyed, black-turtlenecked Holmes gracing the front cover in honor of her presence on its list of the 100 most influential people.

Living the illusion of genius, Holmes drove Theranos to a false valuation of over $9 billion. For a short time, she achieved the fame she sought and was noted as the world's first self-made female billionaire.

Not even egocentrism, confidence, charisma, passion, nor her illusion of control bias could sustain Holmes's fabrication forever. It came to a screeching halt when Captain Holmes was beckoned into port by the SEC, ending her delusional and perilous journey. After a 12-year fantasy cruise, Holmes was indicted for wire fraud and conspiracy.

Her fairytale story was unmasked by *Wall Street Journal* investigative reporter and Pulitzer Prize-winner John Carreyrou, who highlighted the knotted story of Theranos. Carreyrou unraveled the knots for all to see in his book, *Bad Blood: Secrets and Lies in a Silicon Valley Startup.* Then, in January 2022, Holmes was convicted of defrauding investors, and in November 2022, she was sentenced to more than eleven years in prison.

The Deceptive Look and Allure of
the Egocentric Bias: The Halo Effect

The egocentric bias provided a natural runway for additional cognitive biases to latch onto and strengthen Holmes's story. And the Halo Effect loomed large. This bias explains situations where a single individual trait influences how other aspects of a person are perceived. This happens when an overall impression of a person who is, let's say, attractive, engaging, successful, and likable leads one to believe the person also possesses unevidenced traits, such as intelligence and empathy.

Leveraging the halo of her idols, Steve Jobs and Thomas Edison, Holmes sought to create a glowing image of the innovator she fancied herself to be. She transformed herself into a female version of Jobs, adopting his black turtlenecked look, and she strategically planned her photo shoots to mirror photo images of her idol.

Her spellbinding "self" strategy was expertly executed, including her deep tenor voice and ultra-controlled and measured communication, which portrayed her as confident and at ease. Holmes leveraged her alluring look, gaze, voice, and carefully crafted messaging to her advantage. And her audience fell for it—hook, line, and sinker.

Captain Holmes was a masterful marketer and a storyteller, and it worked like a charm. By age 21, she had raised millions and she was referred to as "strategically brilliant." Henry Kissinger, who sat on her board, described her as having an "ethereal quality."

Roger Parloff of *Fortune* referred to Holmes as "remarkable." When the story was unraveling, he said, "You know, I don't know if she's lying, or if it's an unconscious, self-protective, reconstructed reality, but what is coming out of her mouth is not mapping onto reality."

Mind knots were the undercurrent that impelled Holmes *and* her followers to make irrational decisions that triggered irrational actions, ultimately leading to disastrous consequences.

NAVIGATION KNOTS AND TACKS

The Egocentric Bias

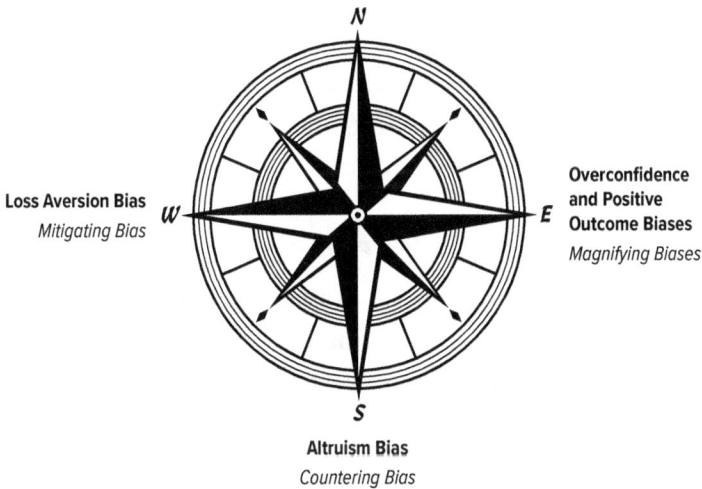

N

Loss Aversion Bias
Mitigating Bias

W

E

Overconfidence and Positive Outcome Biases
Magnifying Biases

S

Altruism Bias
Countering Bias

The Captain's Compass: Captains of Self and Sway

"Detaching from Self-thinking is required to see the bigger picture. Detachment is the natural ego antidote."
—RYAN HOLIDAY, *EGO IS THE ENEMY*

Understanding the unique direction in which biases influence us enables us to reduce errors in judgment and behaviors. This understanding also enables us to use the directional force of biases to our advantage, leveraging a counter-bias strategy.

The Captain's Compass is a navigation tool that illustrates how the directional force of certain biases can *help* captains to mitigate or counter their prominent bias—or *hurt* them by increasing risk due to conspiring biases.

This compass shows egocentric bias at the north cardinal point. Biases shown at the east cardinal point will keep captains on the same risky course, magnifying the negative effects of egocentrism. Characteristics associated with the bias at the west cardinal point, when adopted, can mitigate negative ego effects, reducing risk. Behaviors associated with the south cardinal point bias provide a countering effect, drawing captains in the opposite direction of egocentrism.

The North Cardinal Point: Egocentric Bias

Egocentric bias distorts reality, translating it into a self-inspired perspective. It promotes a "Self is right, and others are wrong" mentality that dismisses others' perspectives.

It invokes overconfidence, exaggeration, and an illusion of control, resulting in overestimating and overrepresenting the ability to perform, control circumstances, and deliver.

The East Cardinal Point: Magnifying Mind Knots

Overconfidence Bias

The Overconfidence Bias impels captains to overestimate their abilities, intensifying the effects of egocentrism. In combination, egocentrism and overconfidence can falsely convince these captains that they can achieve whatever they set out to do.

Overconfidence is sometimes the ego's defense mechanism to combat insecurity. This may seem counterintuitive, though it explains why overconfidence is nearly always hitched to egocentrism. Overconfidence also provides cover for these captains, creating a false sense of importance, skill, and control, strengthening their ability to lure others into their irrational and alternate realities.

Positive Outcome Bias

The Positive Outcome Bias induces people to overestimate the probability of good things happening. This reinforces the egocentric bias, which already produces strong self-achieving beliefs, keeping these captains blindly hitched to an anticipated positive outcome.

Intently focused on her big ideas, Holmes relentlessly promoted her positive dream of revolutionizing healthcare and saving lives. This mind knot magnified the effects of her egocentrism by further obfuscating reality, perpetuating her delusion, and causing others within her realm to abandon logic, rational thinking, and truth in favor of an imagined positive outcome.

The West Cardinal Point: Mitigating Mind Knot

Loss Aversion Bias

Loss Aversion urges leaders to weigh potential costs, risks, failures, and losses more heavily than potential gains associated with a projected outcome. In contrast, egocentric bias causes leaders to overweigh potential gains over threats of risk, cost, potential loss, or failure.

Adopting attributes of loss aversion bias can invoke doubt and caution in the minds of these captains. Research shows a fear of loss will typically override the desire for potential gain. Urging attention toward the cost of failure can be an effective counter to the unchallenged beliefs and false sense of certainty to which these captains are tied, enabling the potential for better balance in thinking and decision-making. On an emotional level, this bias can also be effective in swaying these captains to seriously consider the negative ego and reputational impact they may experience due to a potential failed mission.

The South Cardinal Point: Countering Mind Knot

Altruism Bias

Altruism is others-focused, while egocentrism is self-focused. Given the direct opposition of these two biases, adopting altruistic attributes offers the possibility of moving the dial from self-focused decisions and behaviors to others-focused thinking, representing a countering opportunity for Captains of Self and Sway.

Such awareness allows space to consider the interests and perspectives of others. While altruism in its extreme form would create an entirely new problem for a captain and their organization, in the case of Captains of Self and Sway, any degree of tacking away from egocentrism toward altruism offers a safer route and a more effective outcome option.

NAVIGATING EGOCENTRIC BIAS

Questions: Know your knots

- What is the purpose of my vision, and what would an ideal outcome look like for myself *and* for others?
- What am I doing to acknowledge the contributions and achievements of my team, shifting the spotlight from myself to them?
- Have I sought perspectives from others? Am I genuinely open to feedback, or do I usually follow my own thoughts and direction regardless of what I learn?
- Have I made decisions lately solely based on my perspective without seeking input from others? When was the last time I asked someone on my team how they felt about a decision I made?
- Are the decisions I've been making truly for the benefit of the team and organization, or are they primarily serving my interests?
- Is it important to me to create a sustainable legacy for my organization? What might that look like for me and for others?

Tacking Techniques

- Reflect regularly on decisions and actions, questioning whether you're acting out of self-interest or for the greater good.
- Practice truly listening when others speak—not interrupting, and not forming responses while another person is still talking.

- Regularly solicit feedback on your personal leadership style from diverse sources.
- Trust team members with significant responsibilities to develop trust.
- Involve others in decision-making, ensuring perspectives are considered and unilateral decisions are avoided.
- Form a group of trusted advisors, internal and external to your organization, who can offer candid feedback and diverse perspectives on your leadership and the impact of your decisions.

THE RATIONAL SOLUTION

So goes the leader, so goes the culture.
So goes the culture, so goes the company.
—SIMON SINEK

An egocentric leader can impact the effectiveness of an entire organization. Over time, decision and behavior patterns across the organization will mimic those of the captain. Inevitably, the negative effects of egocentrism are bound to perpetuate dysfunction across the business and even throughout its ecosystem, potentially affecting external partners, vendors, and customers.

What do you suppose would happen if self-focused egocentric leaders *also* demonstrated behaviors associated with selfless altruistic leaders?

What if the altruism bias influenced these captains *in cooperation* with egocentric bias?

When attributes of egocentric bias work in concert with traits of altruism bias, *selfishness meets selflessness*, and the journey completely changes. Breakthroughs occur. Journeys and missions become inclusive, and outcomes are remarkably positive...even extraordinary.

The following story illustrates this pattern. Despite the prominence of this captain's egocentric bias, it was his altruism bias working in concert with his egocentrism that postured him for a lifetime of multiple successes, including the making of a new market.

Ted Turner, The Maverick Man

If only I had a little humility I'd be perfect.

—TED TURNER

Ted Turner was the pioneer of cable news. Referred to as the Maverick Man, he proved to be a Captain of Self and Sway who leveraged the strength of his egocentric bias alongside the altruism bias, which came naturally to him.

Turner was a visionary. While most advised against his big risky ideas and ambitions, Turner remained committed to his thinking and gambled boldly, *knowing* he was right, and others were wrong. Obsessed with winning, he eagerly took risks.

Unlike Holmes, there was substance to Turner's leadership, and he became a proven and successful business builder, leader, and market-maker. His accomplishments are legendary in the media industry and notable in other areas including sports, sailing, environmental issues, and humanitarian achievements.

Far more than a dreamer, Turner demonstrated he was a man of strategic vision and action. He led with uncompromising drive and ambition to bring his visions to fruition. While he respected people who could think for themselves, he was clear that whether in business or at sea, "on a boat there is only one captain."

Under the influence of an emotionally unstable father, Turner developed significant insecurities which stayed with him throughout his life. Believing his father had deliberately instilled self-doubt to ensure he worked harder, he grew to believe every super-achiever shared this vulnerability, causing them to remain unsatisfied and always seeking more.

Alike in many ways, both father and son exhibited self-centeredness, and both suffered from bipolar disorder. While Turner Jr. sustained the same egocentrism and highs and lows as his father, he learned to use the effects of his egocentrism and bipolar disorder to his advantage.

Like egocentrism, bipolar disorder can produce *hubristic pride*—a global sense of self, greatness, and belief in the ability to conquer challenges never faced before. Research shows that bipolar disorder, like egocentrism, has useful traits that can lead to profound accomplishments, mostly in environments where high energy and creativity are an advantage.

Turner demonstrated evidence of this early on while running a branch of his father's business, a small billboard company. He more than doubled profits, proving to be a masterful and confident salesman.

He expanded the company significantly, envisioning that it would deliver information to people more broadly and at any time. Confidently purchasing a small Atlanta station which evolved into Turner Broadcasting System, he pioneered what became known as the "superstation" concept. TBS proved to be the stepping stone to the market he eventually created—cable news.

Rough, Fast, and Furious Seas

An enthusiastic sailor since childhood, Turner's lofty goals took him far beyond satellite signals and into the Pacific and the Celtic Seas. An underdog in the 1977 America's Cup race, Turner once again proved his doubters wrong by successfully defending the America's Cup as the skipper of the yacht *Courageous*.

"Disciplined and outwardly confident," according to Turner's tactician, he famously got in his own way with his unconventional, raucous behavior and unfiltered comments, earning him the name "Captain Outrageous."

Next, Turner took his ego and confidence to the world sea stage, entering the infamous and deadly 1979 Fastnet race. Despite predicted strong seas, and hurricane-strength winds, Turner forged ahead.

Throughout grave conditions, Turner steered the boat by intuition and "feel." Never showing fear, according to his crew, and with conviction and calm, he instilled confidence aboard *Tenacious* as he led her to a bold victory on the world sea stage, in "the worst disaster of 100 years of ocean yacht racing."

Back on land, Turner revolutionized the media business with the creation of CNN, the first 24-hour cable news channel. Confidently, he announced, "We won't be signing off until the world ends." In later years when he was asked how he knew the multiple bets he'd made along the way would be successful in bringing his vision to fruition, he confidently answered, "I just knew it."

Throughout his business ventures, Turner was known as an honest and ethical leader. Leading CNN, he instituted a strict editorial policy to report the news "as is."

Turner demonstrated his financially astute and highly creative mind throughout his business achievements. His ego, intuition, and excellent business acumen led to the merger of Turner Broadcasting with Time Warner in 1996, making the entity the world's largest media company at that time.

When the tide changed following Time Warner's merger with America Online and his divorce from Jane Fonda, Turner rose above his time of crisis, redefining himself as a philanthropist.

Winning and Doing Good: The Difference Maker

"I've gone from a man of war to a man of peace." The truth is there were signs of Turner's altruistic bias throughout his business career. His former associates revered him for "changing the world" with his revolutionary news network, saying, "Ted's business had a human face, a moral face, and a social face. It wasn't just about making money and building an empire."

Turner's reputation expanded from "Captain Outrageous" to "do-gooder" well before his intentional pivot to philanthropy. A decade earlier, he successfully blended patriotism and the will to win in the sports arena when he hosted the inaugural Goodwill Games in 1986 to improve US and Soviet Union relations in response to each country boycotting each other's Summer Olympic Games.

This captain was judged and rewarded on the world stage for his business success, global sailing, and broader social achievements. His many notable achievements include: the first media figure named to *Time* magazine's Man of the Year list in 1991; National Sailing Hall of Fame in 2001; and receiving Humanist of the Year in 1990 from the American Humanist Association.

A passionate environmentalist, Turner devoted many of his hard-earned assets to environmental causes. With the establishment of the Turner Foundation, he issued philanthropic grants for the enrichment of the environment and the population.

Over his lifetime, it's reported Turner has given away over $1.4 billion of his personal wealth, including a billion-dollar pledge to the United Nations. He also signed Warren Buffett's Giving Pledge, promising to give away the majority of his fortune.

"Looking back," he once said, "if I had to live my life over, there are things I would do differently, but the one thing I would not change is my charitable giving. I'm particularly thankful for my father's advice to set goals so high they can't possibly be achieved during a lifetime and to give help where help is needed most."

"I intend to conquer the world," he once told a television-festival crowd in England, "but instead of conquering with bombs, I intend to conquer with good ideas."

Captain Turner is a natural example of the positive effect of what I've named the Egonomic Enrichment Model. He well understood fame and fortune will elevate an ego, but legacy elevates and enriches others across an organization and its ecosystem.

The Egonomic Enrichment Model: The Way Forward

The Egonomic Enrichment Model protects Captains of Self and Sway and their organization from the danger associated with an egocentric-biased culture, instead promoting a culture of enrichment. The model is operationalized through agile practices that leverage certain attributes associated with egocentrism alongside traits associated with the altruism bias—not at the exclusion of either, but rather harnessing the power of both. This is a counter-bias intervention approach.

Egonomic is my term to describe the concept of leveraging the positive attributes associated with ego, such as vision, persistence, and drive, toward the economic benefit of others and the organization by creating positive impact and outcomes both inside and outside the organization. "Egonomic" addresses the upside of egocentrism that can drive and produce positive financial outcomes.

Enrichment refers to focusing on the welfare of others above self. Unchecked, the egocentric bias is concerned with the welfare and enrichment of self above others. The purpose of the model is to transfer the outcome focus from self to others, creating network effects of broader enrichment and value creation.

The power of the model is realized through combining these opposing forces to drive broad enrichment outcomes from the helm to the realm and beyond.

Achieving the Egonomic Enrichment Model

The question is, absent the natural presence of the altruism bias, how can ego-driven Captains of Self and Sway leverage their inherent egocentric attributes to achieve outcomes, leaving a legacy that is personally nourishing, as well as enriching for others?

The answer is by *intentionally* adopting altruistic attributes and behaviors as a means of reshaping purely egotistical behaviors into powerful agents of enrichment beyond the self.

Captains of Self and Sway who demonstrate the mental agility to leverage value drivers of both the egocentric and altruism mind knots in tandem are well-positioned to enrich themselves through the enrichment of others, while leveraging their bold visions, confidence, and positive outcome focus.

From *The Helm* to *The Realm*

While the Egonomic Enrichment Model is important for the captain, it has far greater impact at the organization level. Remember, "As the leader goes, so goes the organization."

THE BOTTOM LINE: ALL HANDS ON DECK

The behaviors of everyone in an organization affect the bottom line. Every behavior has a consequence. Biases influence the behaviors of leaders and, therefore, the resulting consequences.

Given the pervasiveness of mind knots, egocentric behaviors at the top will eventually trickle down to the bottom of the organization...and the bottom line because the leader sets the tone and tenor of the organization.

Business processes and practices are intended to manage behaviors for the benefit of the organization by reducing errors and risk. That is the intention of an Egonomic Enrichment model. By creating awareness of egocentric bias, and instituting appropriate processes and practices, organizations will be better positioned to harness value drivers associated with ego, and value drivers associated with altruism, to achieve enrichment tendencies with broad organizational benefit.

Egonomic Enrichment Model Mission Objectives

- Transfer enrichment focus from self to others.
- Champion culture transformation to an "Enrichment Culture."
- Implement a broad enrichment strategy: Helm to Realm.

The Strategy Equation

Egocentric Bias + Altruism Bias =
The Egonomic Enrichment Model

Turns the rudder from self-focused outcomes to outcomes that enrich others across the organization and business ecosystem.

Strategic Maneuvers and Organizational Guidance: The Egonomic Enrichment Model

Recognizing every organization is unique, the suggestions that follow are intended to serve as guidance, providing choices for Captains of Self and Sway and their organizations to appropriately adapt to their unique operating environment.

The Captain

- Revise the company mission statement and values to reflect commitment to enterprise enrichment objectives.
- Make the company mission a personal mission—not the other way around.
- Engage coaching for personal development and ego management. Develop practices fostering self-awareness, transparency, humility and altruistic-leaning behaviors. Set short-term "ego improvement sprints" to reduce egocentric tendencies. Schedule retrospectives to evaluate progress, address ego-related challenges and to adjust strategies.
- Create enrichment strategies for others inclusive of organization, customers, and markets. Define key metrics related to ego management and others' focus such as the frequency of collaborative initiatives.
- Adopt an enterprise-wide decision process to safeguard against self-serving decisions. Require participation from altruistically inclined business partners.

The Crew—Leadership Team

- Implement quantitative *and* qualitative KPIs to measure financial and non-financial enrichment objectives.
- Develop a formal checks-and-balances feedback tool to discuss and debate new ideas through an enrichment lens with a wide view of the organization, customers, and markets.
- Establish a cadence for leadership meetings fostering consistent perspective exchanges, holding captain and crew accountable for initiatives that drift from the company's enrichment objectives.

- Identify altruistically leaning people across the organization with the strength of character to express dissenting opinions tied to egocentric or self-serving ideas advanced by leadership.

People Processes

- Develop an enterprise-wide egocentric awareness program to heighten awareness and provide training on ego management. Provide training and strategies designed to mitigate egocentrism. Include training on altruism bias, as well as humility, emotional intelligence, trust, and collaboration.
- Implement hiring criteria to identify indicators of egocentric and altruism bias, enabling balanced organizational perspectives in service of the greater good.
- Assess new hires for competent confidence, collaborative and emotional intelligence, and interpersonal skills. Seek people who lift others above themselves. Prioritize gravitas over charisma to elevate leadership strength, integrity, and maturity as an organizational leadership enrichment objective.
- Educate business leaders to practice agile thinking—from a singular financially focused outcome to an enrichment focus, broadening the scope of a successful outcome.
- Implement total rewards incentive packages including financial and non-financial components and prioritize team and organizational successes over individual accomplishments. Uniquely reward individuals in ways that enrich what *they* value, aligning to organization enrichment objectives.

Financial Considerations

- Institute a value capture process to quantify and qualify the "enrichment" value of organizational initiatives. Include value capture in board presentations and leadership meetings to inform decisions for correction and forward momentum.
- Measure the cost of an "Enrichment Mission." Track financial and non-financial costs and create a scorecard that illustrates cost relative to the progress of mission objectives.

Commercial Considerations

- Implement sales training outlining customer-centric objectives tied to enrichment value propositions. Define parameters for pricing and margins ensuring company enrichment objectives are met.
- Develop marketing initiatives and messaging to convey customer enrichment objectives specific to offerings that add value to customers and their end users.
- Create feedback loops to gather market insights and to gauge short-, medium-, and long-term impact of customer and market enrichment objectives.

Board Considerations

- Increase board scrutiny relative to new initiatives and bold ideas presented by the captain, representing a change in strategy and operating plans.
- Require multiple perspectives to reduce egocentric influence at the CEO or leadership-team level.

- Support the captain's effectiveness by aligning altruistically leaning board members to partner closely with the captain.
- Require reporting of both economic and non-economic enrichment objectives in board presentations.

Five Questions to Identify Indicators of Egocentric Bias

1. How would you rate yourself compared to others in your industry and organization? What mistake or oversight taught you the most? How have you adjusted your leadership approach as a result?
2. How do you incorporate the viewpoints and expertise of others in your decision process? How well do your opinions generally align with others' opinions? Are there reasons why you might not consider opposing viewpoints or perspectives?
3. What constructive feedback have you recently received from a team member or colleague? How did you respond, and what actions did you take based on that feedback?
4. To what degree do outside factors influence your decisions?
5. Can you think of a time when you were overly confident in a vision, strategy, or outcome that didn't come to fruition? What would you say went wrong?

TAKEAWAYS: TYING IT ALL TOGETHER

Captains of Self and Sway

Captains of Self and Sway are proud leaders and the holders of the egocentric bias, making them primarily ego-driven and self-focused. These leaders often possess valuable traits including drive, confidence, and commitment that can prove beneficial to an organization—when egocentric bias is managed.

The Egocentric Bias

Egocentric bias causes exaggeration of an individual's opinion and importance while disregarding opinions and importance of others. It influences a self-enrichment focus at the expense of others' enrichment.

Despite its mostly negative effects, this mind knot produces observable characteristics often favored by companies, including vision, confidence, drive, assertiveness, courage, and tenacity—all of which can be positive leadership qualities when egocentrism is managed.

Egocentrism left to its own devices promotes individualistic and self-serving judgment, tangling decisions and behaviors, inevitably resulting in poor and unsustainable leadership, compromising relationships, missions, and outcomes.

The Rational Solution: The Egonomic Enrichment Model

This model leverages positive attributes of egocentric bias in combination with the most productive attributes of altruism bias, enabling these captains and their organizations to counter self and ego, transferring a focus from self-enrichment to the enrichment of others.

THREE

THE CURSE OF KNOWLEDGE BIAS

HOW MANY TIMES HAVE YOU HEARD OR SAID, "KNOWledge is power"?

Knowledge is powerful. But what happens when *knowledge-holders* cannot successfully make the shift to become *knowledge-sharers*?

Is knowledge a source of power when it is tied to its holder?

Is knowledge power when it cannot be shared in a way that others understand?

The answers to these questions are, of course, no.

Why? Because knowledge itself is not where the power lies. The power for any knowledge-holder depends on two critical processes: the effective communication of knowledge and the use of that knowledge in meaningful transformation.

QUIET CAPTAINS OF MORSE CODE

What do I mean by Quiet Captains? These are leaders who prefer to think rather than talk. They are typically introverted with immense depth and resolve. And in their state of "quiet," they think deeply. In fact, they typically become experts in whatever mind journey they pursue.

These calm and critical thinkers make thoughtful decisions with a serious focus on getting it right.

I am also talking about intellectual leaders who are experts in their field, steeped in knowledge and vision.

Now here's the tricky part: though they are often experts, Quiet Captains can struggle with the effective communication of their knowledge. And when they do choose to share their genius, it often requires a fair amount of decoding to be understood by others.

Why? Because their years of compounded knowledge and expertise become the very knot that ties them to their mind's treasure. They often find it difficult to unravel and present their years of knowledge in a way that's easily digestible to those listening.

The combination of "power" and "quiet" may seem like an oxymoron to some. However, it is the special combination of these two distinctive qualities that most often set apart our Quiet Captains. In this chapter we'll examine the Quiet Captains of Morse Code and the prominent mind knot that ties these leaders to their own minds—the Curse of Knowledge.

EXTROVERTED VS. INTROVERTED LEADERS

Research indicates that one-third to one-half of people in America are introverts, and approximately 40 percent of all leaders are described as introverts both by themselves and others.

I recognize that introversion, like extroversion, is not an exact persona. In fact, introversion and extroversion alike encompass a range of intensities.

Susan Cain, author of *Quiet: The Power of Introverts in a World That Can't Stop Talking*, suggests the single most important aspect of personality is where one falls on the introvert-extrovert spectrum. While there are different degrees of "quiet" along the introversion side of the spectrum, for our purposes in this chapter, the Quiet Captains of Morse Code personify introversion in its broadest sense.

One of the most prominent traits associated with these leaders is *quiet*. It is quiet and solitude that facilitates deep thinking, complex problem-solving, and innovation. Yet, the busyness of corporate America is not a kind and welcoming environment for the often soft-spoken, focused-thinking Quiet Captains, Cain also points out.

In most business environments, leaders are expected to have a degree of charisma, vibrancy, and an aura of confidence. Organizations need leaders to be influential, requiring strong communication skills and an adeptness in engaging and inspiring others. Leaders need to be comfortable communicating and leading on the frontline.

Captains with a presence and strong interpersonal and presentation skills are the prized executives in most situations. Look no further than most position descriptions for any CEO or top leadership role. The conventional leadership mandate will describe a leader who would fall on the extroversion side of the spectrum.

But are extroverts really the most effective visionaries and leaders? Winifred Gallagher, science journalist and author of *How Heredity and Experience Make You Who You Are*, writes, "The glory of the disposition that stops to consider stimuli rather than rushing to engage with them, is its long association with intellectual and artistic achievement. Neither $E=mc^2$ nor *Paradise Lost* was dashed off by a party animal."

And yet, extroverted leaders continue to be well-embedded throughout all levels of companies and are prominently found at the helm.

In a rapidly changing world with lots of complex challenges, these conventionally selected extroverted leaders might not always be the best choice. When it comes to critical thinking, companies may be well-served by taking a closer look at Quiet Captains. These leaders offer endurance through their thoughtful and measured approach to logic-based solutions. However, the key to their success lies in their ability to be effective *knowledge-sharers*.

THE CURSE OF KNOWLEDGE AND MORSE CODE

Quiet Captains can spend hundreds of days and thousands of hours pondering every nuance of a given topic or problem. This impressive level of expertise can make it difficult for them to distill their mind's treasure into a level a less-informed audience can understand.

With their minds wound so tightly around their knowledge, these captains typically fail to consider that others have no access to what is stored in their mind. They struggle to untangle their thoughts enough to communicate them to a wider audience, which is the curse of knowledge these captains wrestle with. Unintentionally, Quiet Captains can produce disjointed messaging, even leaving critical information unsaid. This cryptic curse causes these experts to communicate far above the level of understanding of the people to whom they are speaking. They might as well be communicating in Morse code.

THE CURSE OF KNOWLEDGE IN ACTION

The curse of knowledge bias was illustrated through a famous 1990 Stanford University study conducted by Elizabeth Newton. In this study, a "tapper" used their hand to tap a simple song rhythm onto a table to see if a "guesser" could figure out what song they were tapping. The songs were simple and well-known, like Happy Birthday.

Before the test began, the tappers estimated the guessers would be able to correctly identify the song 50 percent of the time. Out of the 120 simple tunes that were tapped, the guessers correctly guessed only three songs, a shockingly low 2.5 percent success rate.

This study illustrates the significant discrepancy between how well the tappers *thought* they could convey the tune and how well they actually did convey it.

And this is the struggle with the curse of knowledge. What may be crystal clear to us is not always easy to convey to our audience.

The curse of knowledge routinely shows up in businesses with abstract language, technical terms, acronyms, and other vague shortcuts people use to cleverly communicate a concept. Communication shortcuts are useful when they are meaningful and clear. However, when shortcuts miss the mark, they tie everyone's mind up in knots! What is clear to the speaker is gibberish to the audience.

An effective communication formula requires knowing the audience, understanding their base rate of knowledge on the topic, and skillfully developing appropriate messaging that will resonate. The only way to be an effective communicator is to be intentional. Often that means dialing back our minds to a *pre-knowing* state, so we can transfer information at a pace and level that meets people where they are.

EINSTEIN'S CURSE OF KNOWLEDGE

In *Made to Stick*, Chip Heath, a professor at Stanford University, and Dan Heath, a senior fellow at Duke University, examine why some messages *stick* while others go unremembered. They call out the curse of knowledge, highlighting the tendency of experts to speak in abstractions when sharing knowledge. These experts forget what it was like when they were novices and fail to design their messaging with a focus on simplicity, resonance, and stickiness.

The Heath brothers maintain that most ideas and messages, even the "less than thrilling ones," can be successfully communicated if properly nurtured and designed. When messages are too abstract, it is frequently because a leader is suffering from curse of knowledge bias.

Quiet Captains of Morse Code who are unaware of this curse routinely fail to put themselves in others' shoes. Instead, as in

Newton's Stanford University study, these experts keep "tapping" while their listeners keep staring blankly back at them, trying to make sense of what they are hearing.

Adam Grant, organizational psychologist at the Wharton School of the University of Pennsylvania and author of *Give and Take* and *Originals,* refers to the curse of knowledge as the "Paradox of Expertise."

Grant references Albert Einstein, who despite his revolutionary published work on relativity, struggled to secure university teaching assignments. When finally given the opportunity to teach his thermodynamics course at the University of Bern, only three students signed up, all of whom were his friends. After a few more "misses" on the teaching front, a friend of his admitted that Einstein "is not a fine talker." Einstein's biographer Walter Isaacson summarized, "Einstein was never an inspired teacher, and his lectures tended to be regarded as disorganized."

Thus, the prized knowledge of these Quiet Captains of Morse Code is their very curse, hitching them to their knowing state. The success of these skilled thinkers rests on their ability to find a strategy that allows them to convert their deep knowledge back into simple, consumable messaging that inspires and advances the power of their knowledge into productive actions of others.

A Recipe For Disaster

Imagine a Quiet Captain of Morse Code who has critical information to share with a leadership team, and who struggles with the curse of knowledge.

The management team will attempt to make sense of the captain's abstract or fragmented messaging. But instead of becoming enlightened, they become entangled in confusion. Fearing they may be alone in their confusion and reticent to ask any questions, they attempt to tie together the strands of information they think they understand, and they fill in the voids themselves. This leadership team then takes their individual distorted understandings of the captain's message and tries to communicate it down through the organization. And so on and so forth. The result: a disjointed and disconnected message that's impossible for the organization to absorb, execute, and deliver upon.

Balancing Solitude and Socializing

Another challenge for these captains is striking the right balance between thinking time and people time. In silence and solitude these thinkers further their genius and creativity. They not only value solitude, they require it. Socializing forces these captains out of the comfort and productivity of their "thinking" zone, and into a much less comfortable "speaking and interacting" zone.

Steve Wozniak, in his memoir, *iWoz: Computer Geek to Cult Icon: How I Invented the Personal Computer, Co-Founded Apple, and Had Fun Doing It*, writes, "Most inventors and engineers I've met are like me—they're shy, and they live in their heads. They're almost like artists. In fact, the very best of them are artists. And artists work best alone where they can control an invention's design without a lot of other people designing it for marketing or some other committee. I don't believe anything really revolutionary has been invented by committee. If you're that rare engineer who's an inventor and also an artist, I'm going to give you some advice that might be hard to take. That advice is: Work alone. You're going to be best able to design revolutionary products and features if you're working on your own. Not on a committee. Not on a team."

We certainly can't argue with Wozniak's success. However, Steve Jobs, with whom he partnered, was highly skilled at effective messaging, which was key to Apple's market penetration and path to success.

And that is where the curse of knowledge can tie these captains down. Their genius can be bound by solitude or the inability to effectively communicate. These captains are often some of the most creative and thoughtful problem-solvers around. But to be effective at the helm, they must figure out a way to balance their need for solitude with sufficient people skills and communication.

Kevin's Knowledge Knot

"The great enemy of communication is the illusion of it."
—WILLIAM H. WHYTE, SOCIOLOGIST,
ORGANIZATIONAL ANALYST AND JOURNALIST

Picture this: a room full of business managers who have been mandated by the CEO of Joe's Best Fasteners to attend a presentation by Kevin, the new Vice President of IT. Kevin was hired to develop an AI and digital strategy aimed at improving operational efficiency.

The CEO believed that Kevin possessed the expertise necessary to elevate his company to the next level.

This was a proud group, highly driven and growth-oriented. They knew the products, they understood their competitive positioning, and they were aware of how each of their products added value to their customer's offerings. There was not much that this group of experts did not know about their business operations.

Except they had no clue about AI or how it might affect their business.

Kevin was the quintessential deep-thinking, problem-solving consultant. While not comfortable in front of a crowd, he thrived in the technology sphere and was known for his ability to quietly develop effective solutions.

After nervously welcoming the business leaders to his talk, Kevin lit up the projector screen and plodded through thirty slides of AI technical terms, buzzwords, and ambiguous references to "Machine Learning in Manufacturing," "Industry 4.0," "smart clouds," and "Industrial Robotics."

With each slide, he was met with a combination of snickers, snide comments, and confused faces.

Kevin's closing remarks sealed the fate of his presentation. "So, as you can now clearly see, manufacturing is entering an exciting next phase with AI. Here at Joe's Best Fasteners, we will be launching our journey with key initiatives, including 'smart factory' digital technology and robotic automation. Thank you. Are there any questions?"

Kevin's audience stared back at him with blank faces. The hum of the air conditioning in the room was all that could be heard.

When Knowledge Becomes Powerless

This Quiet Captain of Morse Code succumbed to the curse of knowledge. Kevin's unrelatable PowerPoint did not facilitate connection with the group, nor did it inform or inspire them.

These thirty slides of bullet points and buzz words did more to turn them away than to draw them in. It silenced them. The message received was the equivalent of Morse code. Kevin should have considered using concrete examples and pictures that would illustrate how AI would improve business. He could have shared simple success stories demonstrating how AI technology has transformed similar manufacturing environments.

Instead, the curse of knowledge presided, and Captain Kevin did not. At the end of the day, the CEO was no closer to achieving his vision but rather found himself on a new mission...damage control.

Failing to empathize with a "beginner's mind" means failing to transfer information with meaning. Without meaning there is no chance for creating emotional connection, inspiration, or transformation. Knowledge becomes powerless.

WHY AREN'T THERE MORE QUIET CAPTAINS AT THE HELM?

Both introverted and extroverted leaders can serve as successful captains. However, when most people think of "strong leaders," they typically envision those with traits associated with an extroverted personality. In fact, one study showed that 65 percent of senior corporate executives see introversion as a barrier to leadership.

In a UC Berkeley study, researchers found that people who are assertive, self-assured, and even forceful are most likely to be hired or promoted to leadership roles. Why? Because these individuals were skilled communicators who spoke up first and answered questions. This gives the appearance of greater competence, even if an introverted leader might actually be the greater expert.

Biased Leadership Mandates

Think about the last time you read a leadership position description detailing the personal characteristics required for the role. It's unlikely descriptors for the executive included, "quiet thinker, soft-spoken, reserved, reflective, introspective, takes time to make decisions, operates with a natural skepticism, prefers written communication over speaking to a group, or avoids social situations unless necessary." I haven't seen it yet.

Sometimes the list will include, "asks tough questions, logical and critical thinker, sets high standards, effective problem-solver, avoids conflict, holds people accountable, and operates with a fervent focus on outcomes." Okay... that's a bit closer to the Quiet Captain. Though, in most cases, the description of the more extroverted leader prevails.

The problem is, even when there's a blend of requirements, Quiet Captains can be outshone by more verbally expressive and charismatic captains.

Logical and critical thinkers require solitude to do what they do, and they're not likely to fit the front stage profile often coveted for top executive roles.

And when Quiet Captains are considered for top leadership positions, critiques usually go something like this: difficult to connect with, unconvincing in ability to influence, paced and measured in conveying thoughts, exhibiting low energy.

A 2009 *Harvard Business Review* study of 4,000 managers across US industries revealed the higher the leadership position, the more likely it is to be held by an extrovert. Mid and lower-level leadership roles, where the requirement for specialized knowledge is more important, tend to be held by introverts. In summary, the higher the position within a corporate hierarchy, the more likely you are to find extroverted individuals at the helm.

Do we really always want to trade our greatest experts for our most outgoing presenters? Or is there a way to help these Quiet Captains unravel their knots enough to be the effective leaders they can be and truly share their wealth of knowledge?

NAVIGATION KNOTS AND TACKS

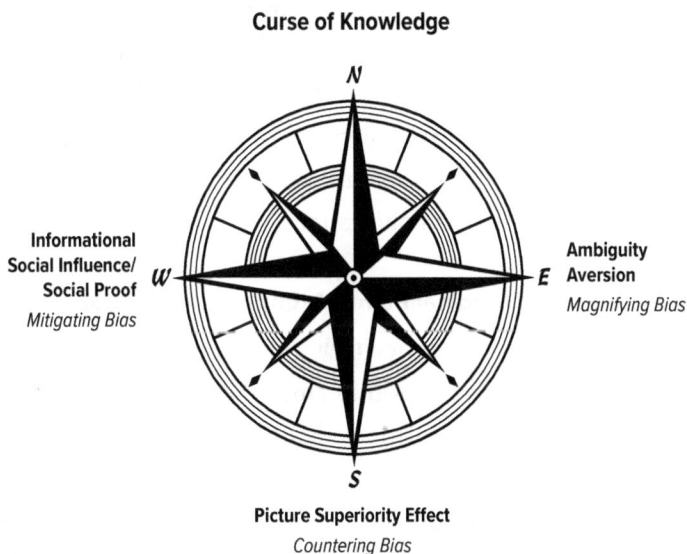

Curse of Knowledge

N

Informational Social Influence/ Social Proof
Mitigating Bias

W — *E*

Ambiguity Aversion
Magnifying Bias

S

Picture Superiority Effect
Countering Bias

The Captain's Compass: Quiet Captains of Morse Code

The Captain's Compass for Quiet Captains of Morse Code can be a useful navigation and intervention tool to improve knowledge transfer with improved communication strategies. Biases at the west and south cardinal points of the compass have attributes that, if emulated by these captains, can improve the clarity and delivery of their message. The bias at the east point, typically a conspiring mind knot, amplifies challenges for these captains, and it too should be managed.

The North Cardinal Point: Curse of Knowledge

The curse of knowledge at the north cardinal point represents the prominent mind knot for Quiet Captains of Morse Code.

These captains must adopt effective techniques and strategies to move their words away from ambiguous and messy messaging to simple and digestible communication that can be delivered to their audience with clarity and confidence. The compass shows ambiguity bias will create more of the same problem. By shifting course and adopting concepts linked to social influence and picture superiority, these captains can significantly improve the effectiveness of their communication.

The East Cardinal Point: Magnifying Mind Knot

Ambiguity Aversion

Ambiguity Effect, also known as ambiguity aversion, describes the tendency to avoid situations that involve a lack of information, ambiguity, or uncertainty.

Failing to consider the *less knowing* state of their audience. leaders predisposed to the curse of knowledge inadvertently use convoluted messaging that is ambiguous and difficult to decipher. In their aim to be clear, minimizing uncertainty, these captains often flood their message with an abundance of information, complex terms, details, and explanations.

Ambiguity aversion urges these knowledge-rich captains to overcompensate in their communication with quantity over quality, making them even less effective communicators and magnifying the ambiguity they aim to avoid.

The West Cardinal Point: Mitigating Mind Knot

The Power of Informational Social Influence

When someone is unable to determine how to behave in a situation, they will often default to what others are doing because they observe *social proof* for the behavior. They assume that the people surrounding them possess more knowledge about a topic or situation than they do, and therefore they are compelled to follow suit.

Social proof is powerful in moving people to action because it reduces friction in decision-making and leverages emotion. Every organization has influencers—those who can stir up emotion, engagement, and the energy to drive action. And social influencers are skilled in the art of effective communication.

A Quiet Captain who struggles to communicate would do well to form a strategic partnership with a skilled influencer who can help them bring their ideas to life. Leveraging this power of Informational Social Influence can be a powerful pivot for captains who wish to circumvent their curse of knowledge pitfalls.

The South Cardinal Point: Countering Mind Knot

Picture Superiority and Simplification

Simplification is key to untangling the curse of knowledge mind knot by effectively moving knowledge from mind to message. However, striking the right degree of "simple" is important. Presentation and resonance of the information will determine whether the message is powerful or powerless. How do these experts go about presenting their genius in a simple way that can be understood?

"A picture is worth a thousand words."

—FRED R. BARNARD, ADVERTISING EXECUTIVE

The Picture Superiority Effect refers to the reality that understanding and retaining information is best achieved through visual imagery.

Allan Paivio's dual-coding theory shows that pictures are superior to words because they generate both a verbal *and* image code in our minds. Images are stored in our memory both in the form of a picture and in the form of words, compounding the odds of understanding and retaining information.

In fact, when concrete visuals are attached to spoken words, retention after three days can be as high as 65 percent, compared to 10 percent retention when information is conveyed through verbal communication alone, according to John Media in *Brain Rules* (2008).

Creating an emotional link is also key to making a meaningful connection. Imagery, stories, and examples that foster emotion make messages relatable and "sticky." Humans are wired to connect to things that elicit emotion, and simple imagery is highly effective.

Quiet Captains of Morse Code can use the picture superiority effect to simplify communication. They can harness the power of pictures to help successfully transfer their expertise to others.

The key is to develop the blueprint for the message *before* attempting to create it. The challenge is to simplify it enough to be understood while still retaining enough complexity to effectively get the message across. To do this, start with these basic questions:

- What does my audience already know about the topic? Am I assuming prior knowledge?
- What do I need them to know?
- Can I explain it simply?
- What questions are they likely to have?
- What do I want them to remember and take away?
- How do I want them to feel?
- What do I want them to do with the information?

The answers to these questions can lend themselves to the creation of effective stories and images that will draw in the audience and help the captain explain complex ideas in simple ways.

Message Matters

In a *McKinsey Quarterly* interview, Chip Heath, co-author of *Made to Stick: Why Some Ideas Survive and Others Die*, commented, "Leaders will spend weeks or months coming up with the right idea but then spend only a few hours thinking about how to convey that message to everybody else. That's tragic. It's worth spending time making sure that the lightbulb that has gone on inside your head also goes on inside the heads of your employees or customers."

Heath added that Steve Jobs always looked quite natural but was known for obsessive amounts of time spent working on new product introductions. He understood that the messaging mattered just as much as the idea itself.

NAVIGATING THE CURSE OF KNOWLEDGE

Questions: Know Your Knots

- Can I explain complex concepts or ideas in a simple, straightforward manner that someone without my expertise would understand?
- Do I regularly ask my team if they understand what I'm saying, and am I open to their feedback and questions?
- Have I tested my communication with someone who is not familiar with the topic to see if they can grasp it easily?
- Is clear and effective communication a priority for me, and am I willing to put in the effort to ensure it happens?
- Do I incorporate visual elements into my communication to help simplify complex information?

Tacking Techniques

- Use a beginner's mind approach. Recall your "pre-knowing" state to guide messaging for those who are not "in the know."
- Empathize with your audience to consider their level of understanding of the topic.

- Message matters. Honor the idea by investing the time to think through the message.
- Use stories, images, metaphors and analogies, infographics, and concrete language to make your message stick.
- Deconstruct to construct. Distill complex concepts into simple, compelling messages using common language and relatable words. Simplify language and chunk information for easier consumption.
- Overprepare without overcommunicating. Create a message "navigation map." Write, organize, and rehearse to ensure fluency and coherence.
- Practice empathy to create an emotional connection for audience engagement and influence. Communicate credibly to build trust and inspire action.
- Review your message with key business partners to gauge its potential consequences and impact. Iterate and refine messaging to improve clarity.

THE RATIONAL SOLUTION

Communication is the currency that enables the power of knowledge. It is the bridge separating knowing from informing, thinking from executing, conceptualizing from commercializing, and prophesying from profiting.

The key to communication that sways people is emotion. Let's take a deeper dive into the importance of emotion in communication by starting with this next story.

Identified as a distant and stiff communicator, former senator, vice president, and presidential nominee Al Gore openly admitted his list of natural talents would not include public speaking. That became a bit of a problem when he had something important to say.

Passionate about tackling increasing climate threats, Gore made many attempts to convey scientific findings that he believed showed serious damage to the environment. Each time, his messaging was ineffective and failed to resonate with his audiences.

Even as a champion of the first congressional hearings on climate change, and a co-sponsor of hearings on global warming, Gore's efforts to raise awareness of these threats gained little serious attention. "I actually thought and believed that the story would be compelling enough to cause a real sea change in the way Congress reacted to the issue. I thought they would be startled too. And they weren't."

His dry delivery and scientific explanation of a small fissure in a distant glacier failed to captivate Congress.

Frustrated by his inability to generate interest and engagement, Gore intuitively created a slideshow of images to tell his environmental story. This Quiet Captain of Morse Code recognized the need to develop messaging that was less technical and more stirring. Projecting simple yet unsettling images, he aroused emotion and interest, successfully transferring his knowledge through meaningful and memorable messaging.

The slide show was a pivotal point in Gore's campaign to increase climate change awareness. Capturing the attention of key influencers, his slides inspired the 2006 film *An Inconvenient Truth*, named best feature documentary at the 79th Academy Awards.

The award-winning documentary, described as a "thought-provoking cautionary tale," had a significant impact and brought attention to climate change. The creatives behind the project masterfully combined Gore's passion and slide show with their filmmaking expertise. Ultimately, they struck a chord with the world. Using their own words, the film was able to make this very confusing issue make sense to people.

Gore initiated a massive communication course correction by crafting an emotional message that won hearts and minds.

Al Gore is an example of a Quiet Captain of Morse Code who advanced in his mission by engaging informational social influencers to simplify and amplify his ideas, knowledge, and message. Translating his knowledge into visual messaging shifted thinking and behaviors and inspired change on a global level.

This Quiet Captain achieved his mission through a powerful version of what I call the Inconspicuous Influencer Model.

The Inconspicuous Influencer Model: The Way Forward
The Inconspicuous Influencer concept follows Al Gore's example: using simplicity, visuals, and social proof to translate knowledge through all levels of the organization.

Despite their proclivity to silence, Quiet Captains of Morse Code *can* be meaningful knowledge sharers, action influencers, and outcome drivers. They can utilize skilled communicators to join them at the helm to enhance their message. They can use visuals and stories to transform complicated, confusing, and tangled talk into simple, compelling, and vivid messaging. They can use simple tools and social partners to translate their knowledge into organizational power.

No longer Quiet Captains suffering from the curse of knowledge, they can be Inconspicuous Influencers. While they still might not love the spotlight, they can do powerful, transformative work behind the scenes and harness the power of their expertise.

From the Helm to the Realm

"Communication works for those who work at it."
—JOHN POWELL, COMPOSER

So, what does this mean for the realms of these Quiet Captains? Organizations are constantly tasked with distilling big ideas, whether technologies, products, or services, into meaningful and relatable messages that others can understand.

Communication is the currency that enables the transfer of knowledge as well as its transformation into powerful solutions.

Leaders, whether consciously or unconsciously, set the culture, tone, and operating rhythm of the organization. Whether in an organization, political arena, or across the globe, communication matters. It is an essential currency in which every leader and organization must be capable of trading fluently to create value.

It's not enough to address mind knots at the helm alone. By enhancing its quality across the enterprise, communication becomes a valuable currency and power multiplier of knowledge—from the helm to the realm.

While the work begins at the helm, the model enables the power of knowledge as a competitive advantage by elevating the currency of communication across the entire enterprise. It offers guidance for stakeholders and organizational engagement.

THE BOTTOM LINE: ALL HANDS ON DECK

Here are suggested strategies to mobilize this model. The framework is intended to be a joint venture between the captain, stakeholders, and the organization.

The Inconspicuous Influencer Mission Objectives

- Convert knowledge possession to effective knowledge transfer.
- Elevate communication effectiveness to transform knowledge into a powerful force for the enterprise.

The Strategy Equation

Curse of Knowledge + Picture Superiority Effect =
The Inconspicuous Influencer Model

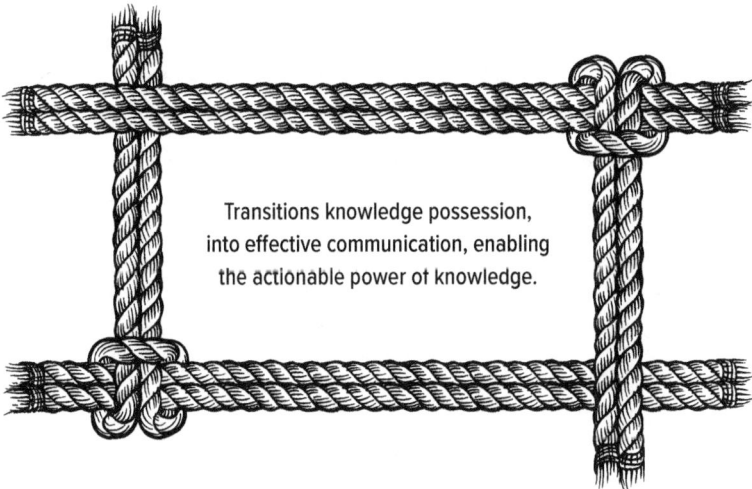

Transitions knowledge possession,
into effective communication, enabling
the actionable power of knowledge.

Strategic Maneuvers and Organizational Guidance:
The Inconspicuous Influencer Model

Consider the guidance below to develop your own systemic plan with agile practices to reduce communication errors stemming from the curse of knowledge bias, while elevating communication as a valuable currency across the organization.

The Captain

- Institute a culture of communication excellence to facilitate effective knowledge-sharing across the enterprise. Emphasize the importance of clear and concise communication as a core competency and critical currency for the organization.
- Identify leadership influencers across the organization, who are skilled information clarifiers, drivers, and inspirers, to serve as message mobilizers and social proof.
- Hire a Chief Communications Officer to champion and institute communication excellence as a core organizational competency. Assess the communication competency level across the organization and outline future state objectives. Define key communication metrics, such as message clarity, engagement rates, or response times, as measures of progress, and to identify areas of improvement.
- Engage a coach to develop authentic relating techniques to improve ability to connect with all levels of the organization.
- Proactively seek social and business "spotlight" opportunities for presenting simple talks to improve comfort level and messaging skills in social and group situations.

The Crew—Leadership Team

- Implement agile practices such as daily stand-ups to ensure alignment and quick response to communication challenges.
- Encourage peer review of important messages or presentations to identify and mitigate potential impact from the curse of knowledge bias.
- Measure the communication pulse of the organization through monthly feedback sessions with team members. Institute a communication cadence with the CEO to connect, communicate, and to share new and evolving information in a simple visual format.
- Implement agile communication tools and platforms that facilitate collaboration, feedback, collection, and real-time sharing of information.
- Ensure use of visual scorecards by function to simplify reporting on key initiatives, KPIs, and challenges to facilitate timely decisions and pivots to operational plans.

People Processes

- Provide continuous feedback and coaching to leaders to enhance their communication skills.
- Implement enterprise-wide training explaining the curse of knowledge and its potential impact to leadership and the organization. Build in a communication training module that specifically addresses the importance of effective knowledge-sharing through simple messaging techniques.

- Tie performance incentives for leaders and teams to their ability to communicate effectively and ensure understanding among colleagues.
- Update recruiting practices, requiring an assessment of communication skills including written, verbal, and presentation capabilities of new hires at every level.
- Establish feedback loops across the organization to capture insights from employees, customers, and other stakeholders on communication effectiveness.

Financial Considerations

- Develop a visual template to convey the financial health of the company in a simple, digestible format.
- Create simple financial models and templates to facilitate decision-making across the business.
- Use agile budgeting and forecasting techniques to adapt to changing business conditions quickly. Promote clear, data-driven communication of financial performance goals across the organization.

Commercial Considerations

- Develop a process to ensure company vision, values, brand identity, and market positioning are clear and consistent across all internal and market-facing communication.
- Apply agile marketing practices to adjust campaigns based on real-time customer feedback. Revisit external communication strategies and narratives quarterly to identify and remedy shortfalls. Collect feedback from customers to assess clarity and effectiveness of external messaging.

- In marketing and sales strategies, prioritize a customer-centric approach that uses visual content and simplification to explain products and services. Invest in client education initiatives that provide clear visual materials to help clients understand complex products or services.

Board Considerations

- Establish a communication cadence to provide updates on strategic initiatives, risks, and opportunities.
- Create a visual dashboard as a critical information-sharing tool leveraging agile reporting focused on key metrics, prioritizing actionable insights over details.
- Use visual imagery to convey clear and succinct messaging of transformation progress toward a culture of "communication excellence."

Five Questions to Identify Indicators of the Curse of Knowledge Bias

1. What strategies do you use to explain a complex topic in simple terms to others with limited knowledge of the topic?
2. How much time do you invest in crafting your message?
3. How do you determine the most important elements of a project or concept, and what do you believe is your most successful approach to transferring your knowledge?
4. Do you have a feedback loop to indicate how well your message was received and understood?
5. What techniques do you use to capture and retain an audience's attention?

TAKEAWAYS: TYING IT ALL TOGETHER

Quiet Captains of Morse Code

These captains are introverted leaders who possess expertise that can be both their blessing and their curse. They are thinkers who operate with logic over emotion. They lead from a position of cognitive strength and with gravitas over charisma. Moving from their "thinking zone" to a "social zone" can be uncomfortable, dreaded, or even disabling. Quiet Captains of Morse Code value the silence of solitude where they can engage in deep thinking to solve problems. Yet, too often, these captains wrestle with the curse of knowledge, inhibiting their ability to effectively transfer their knowledge into an actionable agent of power for their organization.

The Curse of Knowledge

Despite its challenges, this bias comes from a place of deep expertise and understanding which can be an asset if communicated properly. This bias binds leaders to deep-seated expertise and knowledge, constricting their ability to distill and transfer information to others through messaging that is meaningful, relatable, and consumable. Under this curse, leaders believe their communication is clear when, actually, messaging is beyond the understanding of those listening. This curse can be debilitating for Quiet Captains of Morse Code.

The Rational Solution: The Inconspicuous Influencer Model

The Inconspicuous Influencer Model facilitates the effective transfer of knowledge through visual tools and simple messaging, elevating communication into a valuable currency across the organization.

The model's formula ensures the power of knowledge through simplification and visual aids to improve communication effectiveness, transforming these captains from insular intellects to Inconspicuous Influencers. Most importantly, the framework provides a path and guidance for these experts *and* their organizations to harness the power of their knowledge.

FOUR

THE ILLUSION OF CONTROL BIAS

FOR ANY COMPANY TO SUCCEED, THE ACTIVITIES OF its employees need to be controlled, organized, structured, and systematized to an appropriate level.

But what about the leaders who do the controlling? That's a bit trickier.

When it comes to leading and managing employees, who are the most important part of any business, *excessive* control can destroy leaders, missions, and organizations. Leaders must move their visions forward, and rather than commanding and controlling, the only effective and sustainable way to do that is to adopt a mindset of inspiring and empowering.

The Illusion of Control bias can cause captains to overestimate the degree of influence they have over random circumstances, external events, and people. When things don't go as planned, these captains can become frustrated and even angry, especially when the stakes are high. And the more perfectionistic these captains are, the more likely they are to be tangled in their illusion of control.

The illusion of control mind knot compromises the effectiveness of these captains significantly by creating an alternate reality within which they operate, leading them to believe they have far more control than they actually do. It is this lack of realism that capsizes these captains and their ships.

CAPTAINS OF ROPES AND STORMS

Ironically, controlling behaviors are often rooted in the fear of *not* being in control. Leaders who default to command and control seek to protect their authority and *power*, which they believe is achieved through control. It is an obsession with power that often fuels the need to control. Too often these captains believe their power gives them control over the things they fear most— risk, unpredictability, and the *loss* of control, authority, and power. But it's just an illusion. The illusion of control bias, and its commanding attributes, deceives these captains into believing control is the safeguard of power.

Yet with a managed illusion of control bias, these captains can be effective leaders due to their strong outcome focus, and positive characteristics, including determination, perseverance, competitiveness, and results orientation. Outcome-driven, these captains move deliberately and operate with a sense of urgency. They hold others to account and they get things done.

Driven to succeed, Captains of Ropes and Storms will charge toward their goal, potentially damaging people and places along the way. They aim to win, and they operate under an illusion of control.

At a fundamental level, we all seek control—of our time, our activities, our careers, and our lives. Being in control gives us the sense that we have the power to achieve our goals and to create a predictable path to achieve our objectives.

But we're never really in control to the degree we may believe. We may *think* we are, but appearances can be deceiving.

In leadership, the illusion of control bias produces similar illusions of power and superiority. And these illusions manifest in rules, regulations, and restraint, in an attempt to control risk, fear, predictability, and even people.

But *controlling* people is not *leading* people. When people are controlled, they are roped and tied. They become debilitated. Control crushes independent thinking, creativity, innovation, and paths to new ways of working. Control protects the status quo and keeps people running in place.

Control is also the enemy of trust. How can a leader inspire or influence others without earning their trust? And trust isn't earned through control.

Trust Means Ceding Some Control

When a leader trusts, they can cede control, allowing others to perform and achieve. That's because ceding areas of control to others is an act of trust. It demonstrates the leader's confidence in the team and in their ability to deliver. For others to trust a leader, they must believe the leader trusts them to use their minds and skills, to do the work they were hired to do, and to achieve their objectives, even if their approach to the goal might not be the same as the leader's.

When leaders are bound by an illusion of control, there is no trust and no foundation for high performance. In fact, studies show there is an inverse relationship between performance and the illusion of control. This is because this control mind knot is so binding it prevents captains from thinking critically and learning from their mistakes. And control diminishes the morale of those the leader is attempting to control. It debilitates people and destroys both the leader's and the organization's ability to achieve its goals.

In this chapter, we'll explore the Illusion of Control bias through the lens of the Captain of Ropes and Storms—an inflexible and hierarchical command-and-control leader.

The Evolution of Command and Control

In the Industrial Revolution, command and control were an essential feature of leadership. Structure, process, discipline, and perfect execution were overarching drivers of outcomes. Control was critical.

As we transitioned into the knowledge economy, it became clear that innovation was the path to a company's success and sustainability. And that's when command-and-control leadership, in theory, began to become less relevant.

Why? Because control restrains people from thinking outside the box, stifling innovation with overly strict policies, standards, and rules. It prevents creativity and consequently the potential for new business opportunities and growth. Control eliminates the possibility of a workforce that is *intrinsically* motivated.

Command-and-control captains may be effective in delivering execution-focused, short-term business outcomes. However, they often miss the mark when it comes to steering the rudder in the direction of competitive business initiatives critical to the delivery of the longer-term innovative and sustainable business outcomes—essential for survival in a rapidly changing economy.

The digital economy and its open-source models have tested command-and-control leaders even further. Why? Because it has become even more critical to abandon convention in order to reimagine paths to solutions, new ways of operating and serving customers, and critically collaborative ways of working that empower others to steer as well.

To the great frustration of command-and-control leaders, businesses have moved toward customer-centric models that demand an external focus. Consequently, forces outside of the organization are the predominant business drivers, and therefore beyond these captains' control.

DISILLUSIONED CAPTAINS OF ROPES AND STORMS

"Being the leader means you hold the highest rank, either by earning it, good fortune or navigating internal politics. Leading, however, means that others willingly follow you—not because they have to, not because they are paid to, but because they want to."
—SIMON SINEK, *START WITH WHY*

Captains of Ropes and Storms are command-and-control leaders who operate under the illusion they can control circumstances and people.

Control is their modus operandi and it's where they find their power. Their obsession with control is aimed at protecting their power, image, authority, and superiority. While these captains operate through their *self*-lens of perceived power, their lack of self-awareness and self-control more accurately indicates their weakness.

Often, power and privilege enable the illusion of control to become tightly hitched to the character of these leaders.

Patience is not their strong suit. They operate with intensity and instill the same in those along for the journey. With energy, eagerness, and swift movements, these controlling captains can easily become impatient with any crew member who requires hand-holding or who does not keep up with the pace. They have little tolerance for what they perceive to be weakness.

Journeying under the command of these captains is usually tumultuous. Highly domineering, these leaders are usually impatient and short-fused, making them quick to anger.

Because these captains have a clear line of sight to the targeted outcome and how it should be achieved, discipline and structured execution preside over agility and innovation.

When it comes to developing the team, these captains will have earned few stripes. Usually operating with an empathy gap, they are not naturally inclined to give accolades or recognize the contributions of others.

Fearing failure or even the possibility that a lack of competency may be revealed, they will work hard to maintain a strong image, masking areas that may suggest weakness, ultimately leading to even more controlling behavior.

Their illusion of control becomes infused into most of their interactions. They are largely one-way communicators, pushing their words and commands, rather than pulling perspectives from others. Usually direct and argumentative, these command-ers can lack tact and diplomacy.

It should come as no surprise that turf battles are not uncommon for these leaders. Whether passive-aggressive or emotionally blatant, they will defend their territory and their control, reaching into their defense toolbox for anything and any way to circumvent the threat, including driving it out of the organization.

The illusion of control fosters a sense of entitlement and a demand for attention, swaying these leaders to place their own ambitions, feelings, and perspectives well above those of others.

In most cases, these captains direct and control through emo-tion. But not always. Sometimes, they use ropes without rants, restraining people by limiting what they can do and how they should do it.

While Captains of Ropes and Storms typically leverage both the restraint of "ropes" and the emotional force of "storms" to exert their control, those with a more passive-aggressive style will exert their control by restraining with micromanagement ropes.

Micromanagement

"Leaders become great not because of their power,
but because of their ability to empower others."
—JOHN C. MAXWELL

Micromanagement is a common form of restraining and con-trolling. These captains tie their team down by issuing "what" and "how" commands, believing this is an effective way to direct *what* needs to get done, and *how* it needs to be done. In this leader's tangled mind, they are limiting risk, increasing predict-ability, and controlling outcome.

Consequently, people are roped and tied, narrowing their ability to apply their skills beyond the limitations of the directives they are issued. They cannot stretch, grow, or reach their potential. When this is the case, these captains do a disservice to their team, the mission, and their organization. When potential and flexibility are stifled, both individual and organizational improvement are disarmed. Progress and innovation are nearly nonexistent because the organization becomes one of irrational compliance.

These captains use extrinsic motivation to move their organizations to action. They move others toward the goal with an action-avoidance approach, meaning performance is linked to either earning a reward or avoiding some type of punitive response from the captain. This is the "carrot and stick" approach.

Colluding Mind Knots

Mind knots rarely influence in isolation. Rather, similar biases will often band together, intensifying their cumulative effects. I call these colluding mind knots.

Captains under the influence of an illusion of control often have a colluding egocentric bias, both of which have minimal capacity for self-control. These colluding biases create a complex knot for these captains, compounding the odds of negative and ineffective leadership.

The Egocentric Bias

The egocentric bias, highlighted in Chapter 2, is a common colluding mind knot for leaders under the illusion of control. It fortifies the controlling need of these captains, making them insistent that things must be done their way. Despite their ability to get things done, their egocentrism negatively affects those within their path, and ironically, especially those whom they rely on most.

Egocentrism bolsters a sense of entitlement in these captains who believe that with power comes privilege. Over time, egocentrism builds on their fundamental fear of losing control, amplifying their lack of trust, and leading them to develop strategies to stay out in front of others, and sometimes punitive plots to keep others in line...behind themselves.

The Self-Control Bias

Perhaps the most devastating of kinks to the success of these captains is the self-control bias.

Control-obsessed captains spend their days exerting their power and believing they control people and situations when the truth is, the only thing they have the ability to control is themselves. And yet, self-control is exactly where these captains fail.

Why is that?

Because their quest for control and power opens them up to frustration when things go off course and out of their control. These circumstances take them into the clutches of the self-control bias.

The self-control bias causes a *lack* of self-control and a *lack* of self-discipline. Under its influence, when things go wrong and when their illusion of control is threatened, these leaders can quickly lose sight of their disciplined approach to long-term goals. Instead, they react poorly in the moment, compelled by an uncontrolled and undisciplined emotional urge, sending them into a new form of control—damage control.

A lack of self-control is one of the most significant vulnerabilities for these captains, and it translates to poor treatment of others. Raw emotional outbursts and impulsive behaviors result in the alienation and disengagement of teams and a disenfranchised organization, ultimately resulting in negative operating, financial, and business outcomes over time.

The illusion of control is a key trigger for the self-control bias, which hijacks the ability of these leaders to self-regulate, further sabotaging their mission.

Research studies and practical business results show leaders who demonstrate actual self-control tend to achieve good outcomes. Falling prey to the self-control bias, which results in a *lack* of self-restraint and self-regulation, infuses danger and risk into the execution and outcome of their mission.

Elon Musk and Twitter

Perhaps no case study in our time shows more clearly the effects of the Illusion of Control Bias than multi-billionaire Elon Musk's 2022 takeover of the social media platform Twitter.

The story began on January 31, 2022, when Musk began buying shares of Twitter in near-daily installments, amassing a 5 percent stake in the company by mid-March.

On April 4, a regulatory filing with the SEC revealed that Musk had become the largest shareholder of Twitter after acquiring a 9 percent stake, or 73.5 million shares, worth about $3 billion. Before the month ended, Musk reached a deal to buy Twitter for $44 billion and take the company private.

By October, the extent of Musk's desire for complete control of the company became clear when he told prospective Twitter investors that he planned to lay off 75 percent of the company's 7,500 employees. Analysts predicted that with a skeleton staff, there was no way Twitter could maintain any standard of quality. Major corporate advertisers—the source of Twitter's revenues— became skittish about the future of the platform. On October 27, in a message to advertisers, Musk insisted Twitter wouldn't become a "free-for-all hellscape." Few people believed him.

The next day, Elon Musk became Twitter's majority owner.

He fired many top executives, including CEO Parag Agrawal, Chief Financial Officer Ned Segal, Chief Legal Officer Vijaya Gadde, and General Counsel Sam Edgett. It was unclear who, if anyone, would be replacing them.

As for content moderation, Musk announced, "Twitter will be forming a content moderation council with widely diverse viewpoints. No major content decisions or account reinstatements will happen before that council convenes."

On November 4, Musk began mass layoffs aimed at cutting roughly half of its 7,500-person workforce "as necessary measures to cut costs and save the company." The separated employees were notified by email.

On November 10, Musk warned employees that Twitter did not have the necessary cash to survive. The company was running a negative cash flow of several billion dollars, said Musk, without specifying if that was an annual figure. He mentioned the possibility of bankruptcy.

The next day, CNN's Brian Fung wrote, "Two weeks after Elon Musk completed his acquisition of Twitter, the future of the company has never looked less certain. In the past week alone, one of the world's most influential social networks has laid off half its workforce; alienated powerful advertisers; blown up key aspects of its product, then repeatedly launched and un-launched other features aimed at compensating for it; and witnessed an exodus of senior executives."

Insiders described this Captain of Ropes and Storms as dismissive of accountability, even in the face of scrutiny by the Federal Trade Commission, which publicly warned in a rare forward-looking statement that it was "tracking recent developments at Twitter with deep concern."

At the time of this writing, the future of X (formerly Twitter but renamed by Musk), is unclear. One thing is certain: Elon Musk took control of the company, and as he charges toward his bold vision, his illusion of control bias cannot be mistaken.

NAVIGATION KNOTS AND TACKS

"Instead of worrying about what you cannot control,
shift your energy to what you can create."
—ROY T. BENNETT, *THE LIGHT IN THE HEART*

By becoming familiar with this Captain's Compass and the tacking techniques below, Captains of Ropes and Storms can navigate away from the gales into which their illusion of control urges them, instead steering into safer waters.

Illusion of Control Bias

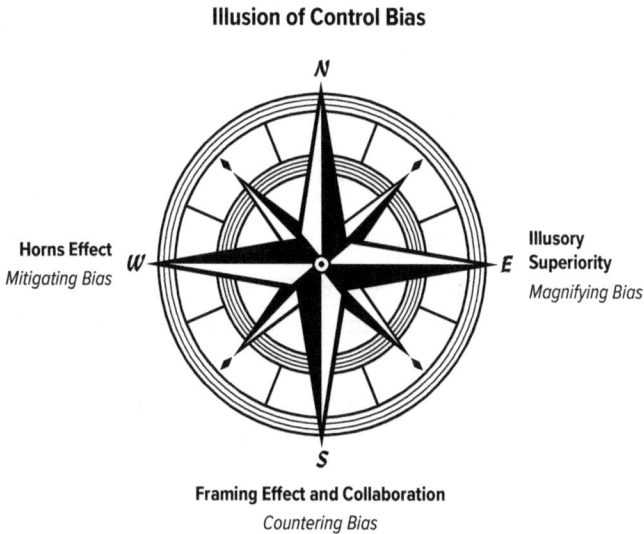

The Captain's Compass: Captains of Ropes and Storms

The North Cardinal Point: The Illusion of Control

The Captain's Compass for Captains of Ropes and Storms shows the illusion of control bias prominently positioned at the northern cardinal point, indicating it as the primary mind knot for these captains. Possible improvement tacks for these captains are found at the west and south cardinal points, while the east cardinal point mind knot promises more risk if not managed.

Let's take a look at the key magnifying bias for these captains, the Illusory Superiority mind knot.

The East Cardinal Point: Magnifying Mind Knot

Illusory Superiority

Illusory superiority persuades these leaders to view themselves as superior to those around them. This mind knot leads these captains to overestimate their desirable qualities relative to others, whether intelligence, confidence, or other "superior" characteristics, while underestimating their undesirable traits and regarding others as inferior. Illusory superiority not only gives these leaders an irrational sense of superiority, it amplifies their illusion of control.

While no leader can achieve their mission alone, they can derail it by believing they can control it. Illusions of control and superiority, working in tandem, are outcome- and culture-killers.

The West Cardinal Point: Mitigating Mind Knot

The Horns Effect

In Chapter 2, we saw Elizabeth Holmes leverage the influence of the halo effect, positioning herself within the glowing "halos" of Steve Jobs and Thomas Edison, swaying others to associate her with the positive characteristics and achievements of her idols.

The horns effect is the opposite. This bias casts a negative shadow effect instead of a glowing halo effect. For these captains who value their image and their position of power and control, the horns effect is a threat.

Yet it's the threatening nature of this bias that can influence behavioral course correction for these captains. Stemming from their illusion of control, Captains of Ropes and Storms are prone to overcontrolling others and under-controlling themselves. In each case, they default to uncontrolled negative behaviors and emotions, creating their own self-defeating horns effect.

The shadow-casting threat of the horns effect can urge these captains to take command of what they can control—themselves.

Remember, these leaders value control of their position, power, and image. The horns effect can urge these captains to redirect their course by taking conscious command of their emotions and behaviors, lifting the shadow and threat of the horns effect and its damaging consequences. This intervention requires these captains to direct their inclination to control toward themselves in the interest of self-preservation.

The South Cardinal Point: Countering Mind Knot
Framing Effect

The southern cardinal point of the compass represents a potential countering course for these captains, provided they can manage the mental bending required to shift from their natural course of thinking with the framing effect.

The framing effect can influence and inspire action based on the way in which information is presented. People will draw different conclusions from the exact same information depending on *how* the information is shared, or *who* shares it. The framing of the message activates unconscious triggers that affect the way others process and respond to the message.

In this case, the "framer" is the leader. When a leader masterfully frames a position, using words that evoke positive emotion, they can inspire others to act based on the power of emotion instead of the illusory power of their commands.

When controlling leaders issue directives and commands focused on *what* others should do and *how* they should do them, the response is generally negative emotion—rarely an effective influencing approach.

When these leaders take the time to frame their directives within the context of *why* instead of *what* and *how* commands, they can tap into the power of intrinsic motivation and move away from their less effective, extrinsic "carrot and stick" motivation approach.

Instead, these leaders can use the framing effect to their advantage by presenting their mandates within a frame of words that explain why the mission and mandate are important, what the person can do to advance the mission, and how they will feel when they accomplish it. Understanding the framing effect and its powerful influencing approach can move these captains from commanding and insistent to empowering and inspiring leaders.

Trust, Collaboration, and Empowerment

Control aims to preserve self through power and authority. In contrast, collaboration aims to engage and empower others through the power of others' participation. Collaboration and empowerment require trust to give away power, control, and even authority.

When these captains can see their way clear to "reframing" how they can satisfy their attachment to power and their sense of control through trust, collaboration, and empowerment, they can manage their illusion of control more effectively, while reaping the reward of empowering others.

While their illusion of control can never be eradicated, how captains think about control and authority can be shifted. The key for these leaders is to reframe their thinking by recognizing that any movement in the direction of a calmly controlled and collaborative approach would go a long way toward elevating and enhancing their image, effectiveness, and actual power in the eyes of their followers.

When these captains understand that sharing power is a more effective and sustainable path to actually *having* power, they will inspire support for an extended reign at the helm.

NAVIGATING ILLUSION OF CONTROL

Questions: Know Your Knots

- Do I generally believe I can control or change a situation or outcome, even in complex circumstances?
- When evaluating a situation, do I actively seek input from others, or do I rely solely on my own judgment and decisions?
- Do I often use the terms "influence" and "control" interchangeably, failing to recognize that I can influence outcomes to some degree but not control them entirely?
- How often do I micromanage others because I believe that my control over every detail is essential for success? When things don't go well, do I stay in conscious command of my emotions?
- Am I willing to adapt my plans and strategies when it becomes clear that the situation is not under my control as I initially believed?

Tacking Techniques

- Make the "why" of the mission clear. Identify what winning represents for the business and the team. Foster collaboration by framing shared goals and benefits.
- Reframe controlling a situation to *controlling a response* to a situation. Recognize what you can and cannot control.

- Monitor self-control and emotional output. Make a list of emotional triggers *and* strategies to avoid or manage them.
- Practice being receptive instead of reactive, and trusting instead of controlling.

THE RATIONAL SOLUTION

Captains of Ropes and Storms have the potential to be strong leaders due to their multiple compelling attributes, including decisiveness, confidence, determination, sense of urgency, and an unwavering drive for results. However, the journey for these captains is not without complications.

A quick review of key manifestations and consequences of illusion of control bias include:

- Overconfidence and excessive risk-taking leading to financial losses.
- Overestimating the ability to control, leading to misconceptions of outcomes.
- Being reluctant to delegate, leading to micromanagement, and trust issues.
- Attributing positive outcomes solely to the leader's own actions, known as attribution errors.
- Blaming others or external factors for negative outcomes rather than accepting responsibility.
- Strained relationships due to an empathy gap, lack of trust, and a lack of self-control.

- Control-driven leadership leading to a debilitating environment driven by fear and void of creativity and innovation.

So, what can these captains do to ensure the success of their mandate when the illusion of control and its ancillary kinks are likely to undermine their mission?

Reversing or tempering an illusion of control in these captains is difficult given their strong attachment to power. The way these captains can get out of their own way is to *get into the minds of others*.

Martha Stewart: The Double-Layer Market Baker

*"I think you can fairly say I spawned or laid an egg
that has turned into a lifestyle industry."*

—MARTHA STEWART

In the 1990s, Martha Stewart knew all the right ingredients to successfully bake, decorate, and frame the homemaker lifestyle industry. Her success was homemade, and it was the result of a blend of attributes including command, control, confidence, competency, commitment, and creative connection. Mix in a lot of ambition, business acumen, framing, and inspiration, and there you have it, a platter of delicious homemaking that her audience gobbled up.

Transforming the notion of homemaking from necessary and uninteresting to meaningful and magnificent, Stewart flipped and framed an inconsequential homemaking market into a meaningful cottage industry, leveraging her economic savvy, commanding drive, and crafty charm.

Martha gave homemakers the "why" and the "how," which resulted in Martha Stewart Living Omnimedia, Inc. becoming a leading integrated content company dedicated to enriching the lives of women and their families.

With four divisions including publishing, television, merchandising, and direct commerce, the company aimed to make "every day more meaningful, more functional and more beautiful." This was done through the dissemination of inspiring ideas and products to "elevate the familiar elements of daily life, infusing them with the pleasure and confidence that comes from the growing sense of mastery and discovery we foster in our customers and ourselves." Martha Stewart's perfectionistic drive ensured all company offerings were high quality and content was "timeless."

Martha Stewart Living Omnimedia Inc., was valued at approximately $2 billion after Martha took the company public in 1999.

Martha has certainly been called out for her domineering, bossy, and emboldened character. We might describe this self-made Captain of Ropes and Storms as a double layer cake. Beneath the beautifully iced, charming, and alluring layer of Martha, which inspired and warmly invited the world in for a taste, was a hidden layer that controlled and supported "Martha" the entrepreneurial, controlling "domestic media maven," as some referred to her. Neither layer of Martha on its own could have accounted for her impressive success. Through artfully leveraging the best of both, Martha Stewart baked up an empire.

"I'm a maniacal perfectionist," she has said about herself.

Perfectionism escalates the intensity of the illusion of control mind knot. Both perfectionism and control are born from similar fears of failure, powerlessness, and compromised self-image.

Like most perfectionists who hold themselves up to near-impossible standards, Stewart's expectations were no less for those whom she employed, or for those with whom she collaborated in business. Known for becoming enraged when her ingredients requests were not exact or when it came to any other detail that was less than perfect during one of her televised sessions or magazine shoots, Martha knew best and *insisted* it be done her way.

Though Captain Stewart proved to master the art of control across her business life, the illusion of control got the best of her in her personal life. First, her relationship with her then-husband of twenty-nine years spun out of control, resulting in the end of their marriage. Allegedly berating her husband on a consistent basis, he eventually jumped ship.

Her well-publicized, less-than-perfect handling of her brush with the law in 2001, which resulted in a five-month prison sentence, also proved a departure from her illusion of control. Selling $230,000 worth of stock in drug company ImClone Systems the day before that stock plummeted, Stewart was tried on charges related to insider trading. She was found guilty of conspiracy, obstruction of justice, and securities fraud linked to the stock trade.

While Martha pleaded not guilty, the indictment represented Stewart as trying to control the facts by going out of her way to cover up the circumstances of the sale of the shares. It was revealed that Stewart crafted a tale of a previous agreement with her stockbroker to sell the shares if their market value fell below a predetermined price. The indictment also revealed an altered phone message from her broker "immediately following a lengthy conversation with her attorney."

Captain Stewart could not control the immediate impact on her business because of her legal misstep, nor could she control the decline of the publishing industry in the late 2000s. She sold her company to Sequential Brands Group for far less than it was worth at its peak.

No one can deny Stewart created a lasting mark in the lifestyle and media industry and in millions of households across America. And she presses on. Now in her eighties, she continues to create new businesses and her entrepreneurial spirit and self-branding are alive and well.

In addition to her Home Collection selling through Wayfair and a Martha Stewart launch on QVC, which is an educational format with a retail purpose, Stewart also released a new book titled *Martha Stewart's Organizing: The Manual for Bringing Order to Your Life, Home & Routines.*

Stewart masterfully flipped her power into personal authority. Instead of telling people what to do, she put herself in the collaborative and inspiring role of supporting and contributing to the mission of her audience—a better lifestyle.

While many commanding leaders value individual advancement over people, Stewart brilliantly crafted a path to her individual advancement through *inspiring people while advancing their personal aspirations.*

She said, "There are two kinds of people...There are the dreamers who go and buy, and there are the doers who go and make. And I've always recognized that. So, the dreamers are what support our company because they will buy the product that they could make if they wanted to, had time to, or were so inclined to."

Stewart intuitively figured out how to leverage her addiction to herself, power, and control, while inspiring and collaboratively supporting and giving "power" to her audience, who she knew would benefit personally from her expertise. She recognized that others, once inspired, would be the way forward to achieving her goals, fame, and fortune.

Captain Stewart is a natural example of the Insistent Inspirer Model.

The Insistent Inspirer Model: The Way Forward

The Insistent Inspirer Model can change the game for Captains of Ropes and Storms, allowing the authoritative nature of these captains to move people to action, and satisfying their urge to control by reframing instructions into inspiration. At the same time, the model allows these captains to increase their power by giving power to others. This leads to strong outcomes for the captain, the organization, and the business.

The model recognizes the positive aspects of the value drivers associated with illusion of control including determination and ambition. When these leaders pair the framing effect with their illusion of control mind knot, they can cast their directives in a way that speaks to others in a compelling manner that resonates, motivates, and inspires.

Using the framing effect to present information in a way that reduces the perception of control, these captains can frame decisions as opportunities for collaboration and shared ownership. Framing the *why* of the mission transforms diminishing directives into inspiring ideas that foster empowerment and collaboration across the organization. The model requires the *courage* to move from a top-down directive approach to a horizontal, inspiring empowerment approach.

Why? Because the actual power of these leaders rests on the spirit of the people they empower. Tapping into the ambitions of others is the key to achieving the true power and outcomes these leaders seek.

This model enables these forceful captains to focus on both self-interest and others-interest, by shifting their power from *personal control*, from which others retract, to *personal authority*, to which others gravitate—and from which they draw inspiration, confidence, and their own power to achieve. This show of authority empowers others and mobilizes them toward goals. It enables these captains to be leaders of intrinsically motivated and inspired people, rather than "bosses" of resistant, fear-based task doers.

THE BOTTOM LINE: ALL HANDS ON DECK

While the Insistent Inspirer Model is important for these captains, it has far greater impact at the organization level.

Creating awareness is only the first step to a rational solution. Strategic and organizational tactics and processes are required for systemic and sustainable change.

The Insistent Inspirer Model Mission Objectives

- Transform command-and-control leadership into accountable and inspirational leadership by intrinsically motivating others.
- Inspire, engage, and empower, elevating leadership and organizational effectiveness.

The Strategy Equation

Illusion of Control + Framing Effect and Collaboration =
The Insistent Inspirer Model

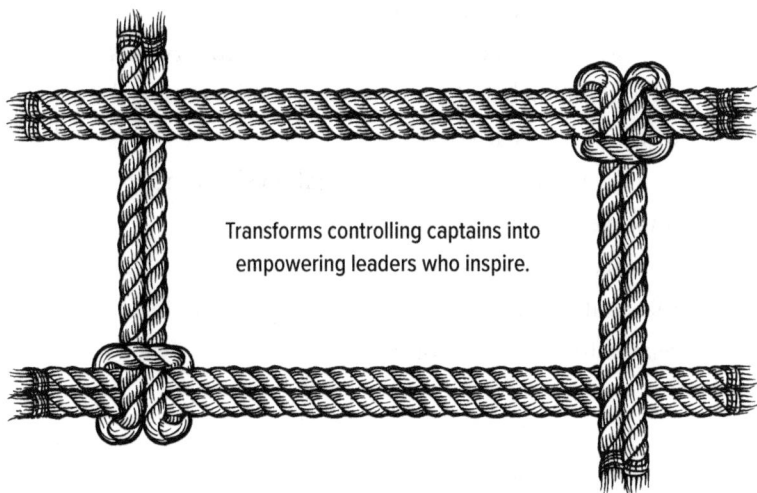

Transforms controlling captains into
empowering leaders who inspire.

Strategic Maneuvers and Organizational Guidance:
The Insistent Inspirer Model

The Captain

- Practice collaboration instead of control. Own the vision,
  communicate goals and expectations, engage others
  on strategy, and empower the team to create the most
  effective navigation plan to inspire collaborative execution.
- Engage in scenario planning to prepare for various
  possible outcomes.
- Position *directives* within inspiring frames by sharing
  information that empowers and moves others to action,
  building trust and tapping into their *why*. Think *influence*—
  not control.

- Practice transparency. Respectfully hold people accountable to performance objectives. Track successes resulting from trusting and empowering others.
- Recruit or identify an existing business partner with a strong conscious command of emotions to serve as an advisor and behavioral model for providing leadership direction and self-control.
- Engage a coach to enhance delegation skills and to improve micromanagement tendencies.
- Identify triggers of emotional missteps. Set short-term "self-control improvement sprints" with clear objectives related to emotional control.

The Crew—Leadership Team

- Develop diffusion strategies to counter the captain's commanding style.
- Shift the captain's focus from managing details to leading strategically toward outcomes.
- Ensure context accompanies directives, including the importance of the activities to achieving objectives.
- Conduct pre-mortem exercises where you imagine an initiative has failed and analyze the potential causes, including those beyond your control.
- Adopt metrics related to collaboration, autonomy, and decision-making effectiveness.

People Processes

- Champion the use of agile collaboration tools and platforms that facilitate autonomy, open communication, and teamwork.

- Develop a company-wide training program to guard against an illusion of control culture. Include modules focused on the illusion of control, emotional control, delegation, collaboration, perfectionism, and trust.
- Develop non-financial incentives, including leadership and management opportunities, at all levels of the organization.
- Develop a leadership and management training program focused on "intrinsic motivation"—what it is and why it's important. Train leaders how to identify and tap into intrinsic motivation as an effective strategy for both individual and business performance.
- Establish feedback mechanisms that allow employees and stakeholders to challenge instances of micromanagement or control-related behaviors.

Financial Considerations

- Develop a measurement and reporting tool designed to illustrate the impact of the illusion of control and its resulting behaviors on financial and business outcomes. Draw insights and provide recommendations of approaches to foster calculated risk and improve outcomes.
- Support the captain's vision and strategic objectives through financial transparency, illustrating the positive impact of an empowered and collaborative organization.
- Implement data-driven processes that reduce the need for excessive control.

Board Considerations

- Provide guidance through collaborative discussions addressing potential business risk associated with overcontrolling, while highlighting business opportunities gained through empowerment.
- Encourage the board to focus on strategic guidance rather than attempting to control operational details.
- Insist on inspiring framing for a steadier path to strategic goals, including commitment to a milestone map to demonstrate progress toward long-term objectives.
- Monitor and assess the captain's decision process, identifying the impact of the illusion of control.

Five Questions to Identify Indicators of Illusion of Control Bias

1. Can you share an example of when you claimed credit for an outcome that might have been beyond your control?
2. What is your approach to motivating your team toward pursuing your vision?
3. What strategies do you use to develop a culture of trust across your team and organization?
4. How often do you actively seek out opportunities to influence outcomes even if it is unlikely to have an effect?
5. Are you more likely to take risks when you feel like the outcome is within your control?

TAKEAWAYS: TYING IT ALL TOGETHER

Captains of Ropes and Storms

When bound by the illusion of control mind knot, these leaders believe they can control people, performance, situations, and outcomes.

Often entangled in a need for power, these leaders fear uncertainty, risk, and a loss of control. Their illusion of superiority complicates their leadership further by accentuating themselves and demanding admiration and compliance from others.

Captains of Ropes and Storms become easily unraveled when circumstances are out of their control. This causes frustration, high emotion, and a loss of self-control. Influenced by an illusion of control, these captains alienate teams, disenfranchise organizations, and compromise outcomes.

The Illusion of Control Bias

Illusion of control bias reflects an addiction to power and self. This mind knot encourages a "taskmaster" style of operating. It convinces these captains they can control others, as well as situations that are well beyond their control.

The Rational Solution: The Inclusive Outcome Model

This model provides a framework and path to inspirational leadership and achieving outcomes. The model represents an agile counter-bias approach, requiring the integration of key value-driving attributes associated with illusion of control bias, including accountability, discipline, and a drive for results, with the proper framing effect, collaboration, empowerment, and trust.

FIVE

THE CONFORMITY BIAS

ACCORDING TO MULTIPLE RESEARCH STUDIES, MOST people are conformists. We do certain things because we see others doing them. Sometimes we conform even when we don't exactly know if the things we are doing are good or make sense.

THE CONFORMITY BIAS

*"What is right is not always popular, and
what is popular is not always right."*
—ALBERT EINSTEIN

Conformity is a social bias that compels people to fall in line with group norms. It causes people to look to a group for guidance when they feel they don't know any better. Even when they are knowledgeable, they may choose to conform either explicitly or by omission to avoid rocking the boat and for fear of social rejection.

There are multiple factors that influence conformity, including group members' status or the group's size and cohesion. Even when those with lower status in the group have an opinion about what is right, they will often remain silent, thereby agreeing by omission. Or they'll simply go along with the position of the higher-status members to remain in good standing with the group. With no dissent expressed, group members believe they are all in agreement, creating an illusion of consensus.

Internal factors also come into play, including the individual's level of security or insecurity. This is an important point, because the greater the number of people who are challenged with feelings of insecurity, the greater the likelihood they will ignore their own conscience and go along with the group's common thinking.

Conformity creates a comfort zone. To fit in and avoid the discomfort of straying from common thinking, most people will adopt norms without much thought. At a societal level, conformity is generally a good thing, enabling people to fit in and function effectively within a social or community context. The alternative can be chaos.

On the flip side, conformity causes people to trade their individuality for acceptance, compromising their personal identity. And because conformity encourages dependency on the majority, it diminishes independent and diverse thinking. A sense of belonging is a basic human need. But often, the need to belong further strengthens the gravity of conformity thwarting personal, professional, and organizational progress.

There are different faces of conformity to consider.

Compliance, its most benign form, occurs when an individual adapts their behavior publicly, to align with a group's expectations, though privately they remain tied to their personal beliefs. This form of conformity is temporary and linked to the situation or to the duration of group pressure.

Identification occurs when an individual adopts beliefs and behaviors of a like-minded group to establish a relationship with the group for the positive status or value they will gain through affiliation. Identification offers temporary conforming change because it is tied to association with the group which may not continue.

Finally, when an individual changes both their behavior and their beliefs, their conformity is internalized. *Internalization* reflects true acceptance of group beliefs and behaviors extending beyond an association with the group. The behaviors and beliefs are integrated by the individual becoming part of their self-concept.

In the context of business, conformity can be the killer of significant progress, change, and innovation. Depending on the extent to which conformity permeates the culture, it can bring about a company's slow death. Change cannot happen when people are not willing to rock the boat.

CAPTAINS OF ALL HANDS AND MINDS

Captains of All Hands and Minds value agreeableness and unity. Their hallmarks are loyalty, compliance or identification, and a strong attachment to tradition. Consensus-driven, these leaders identify as servants of the organization, striving to maintain the stability of strong social structures. As such, they often have a *form over function* drive, favoring consensus as an operating structure and social form, while compromising the functionality of good judgment and reasoning in decision-making.

Conflict-averse and with well-developed people skills, these consensus-driven leaders may fancy themselves as inclusive by bringing diverse people into the room.

Not so fast!

Asking people to have a *hand* in an effort, without sharing their *mind*, is not being truly inclusive. Having a diverse group of people does not guarantee they're all valued as individuals with unique perspectives.

There's a difference between *diversity* and *inclusion*. Put simply, diversity is about the "what." It focuses on diverse backgrounds, experiences, orientations, capabilities, and perspectives. All good things for a team. Achieving diversity is a good first step—but it's *only* the first.

Inclusion, on the other hand, is about the "how." It's about how a diverse group is valued and enabled. Inclusion is a measure of how an environment empowers people to actively participate with their minds and thrive for the benefit of both the individual and the organization. Diversity without inclusion is nothing more than illusion.

When *consensus* is a forced goal in any decision-making process, inclusion is mostly an optical illusion, not the opportunity it's meant to be. Driving a forced consensus leads to conformity, mostly rooted in compliance or identification, which is unsustainable and rarely in an organization's best interest.

Unless individuals can contribute their unique perspectives, they are not truly included in the group. And that's when the concept of diversity and inclusion becomes the reality of conformity, groupthink, and the *illusion* of consensus.

Culture of Consensus

"Whenever you find yourself on the side of the majority, it is time to pause and reflect."

—MARK TWAIN

Consensus generally means agreement on a group decision with no lingering objection. For some organizations, consensus is revered as a prized cultural value. Some might assert that consensus is an obsession to which their company culture is tethered. Why? Because it is associated with inclusion and agreement, suggesting the perspectives of group members are represented and viewpoints are unified. Now, that sounds good and seems logical—but that's not the way it usually goes.

Achieving agreement among a group of people is challenging. The larger the group, the larger the challenge.

The way in which consensus is achieved warrants examination.

There's a difference between valuing consensus as an inclusive *process* or as a targeted *outcome*. Consensus as a targeted outcome overrides the purpose of the decision-making process—the business objective for which the decision is being made. Valuing consensus as an outcome places the optics of agreement above business objectives.

And when the act of reaching consensus is the absolute goal, the decision-making process is usually *exclusive*, rather than inclusive. The appropriate group members may be invited into the room, and there may be plenty of diversity represented, yet their voices may never be heard, resulting in a decision arrived at in the absence of a diversity of thought and voice. Usually, this is because of conformity bias.

In this chapter, we explore the mind knots of conformity and its close cousin, groupthink, through the lens of Captains of All Hands and Minds—consensus-driven leaders.

Sameness and the Status Quo

"A genuine leader is not a searcher for consensus but rather a molder of consensus."
—MARTIN LUTHER KING, JR.

In *Outsmart Your Instincts*, authors Hansen, Harrington, and Storz point out the common concept, "Change is bad, same is good... It's in our nature as humans to non-consciously believe that whatever situation currently exists is better than what doesn't exist. We overvalue what we have compared to what we could create...Not doing something is the omnipresent option, always ready to assert its attractiveness."

Captains of All Hands and Minds value tradition and, often, symbolism. Holding traditional values in place, such as a tie to consensus, these leaders may strangle a mission or strategy, and ultimately the company's progress in the interest of the status quo.

Sameness is another facet of the status quo. Perhaps you have witnessed or even been guilty of hiring people who seemed like you, and who seemed to match your organization's vibe. Their sameness gave you a level of comfort, swaying your decision to add them to your team. Hiring in one's own image is all too common. It feels comfortable and safe.

But sameness fosters conformity and empowers the veil of consensus—the exact opposite of cognitive diversity.

Consensus objectives subconsciously influence conformity of thought.

When you really think about it, while many would say consensus is "inclusive," rather, it is often the epitome of exclusivity because it can force sameness. On the topic of culture and hiring for "fit," Glenn Lopis, a *Forbes* contributor, wrote, "That's not diversity of thought. That is a system for making sure people conform. It is an environment that does not allow us to practice the skill of getting along with people who are different from us. It's a corporate culture that values efficiency above innovation and values the corporate brand over individual contribution."

While Captains of All Hands and Minds may publicly acknowledge the value of diverse perspectives and genuinely appreciate others' unique value, they often create scenarios of lost opportunity because of their strong commitment to consensus. These captains are naturally inclined to sail with the wind, not against it.

Consensus and the Endowment Effect

The Endowment Effect is an emotional bias grounded in feelings associated with ownership. The research behind the bias highlights the two main psychological reasons that cause this effect. The first is *ownership*—we value what we own more than what we don't own. The second is *loss aversion*. We tend to stick with something that may be inferior or unprofitable because the prospect of exchanging it for an alternative is rightly or wrongly not perceived to offer more value.

This effect explains why Captains of All Hands and Minds develop an affinity for consensus in principle. They tie themselves to consensus because within the context of their organization's consensus culture, they bear a sense of ownership for it.

This mind knot is powerful because it urges a strong attachment to emotion and symbolism. It causes these captains to bind themselves to a consensus objective at all costs, as the *owners* of driving consensus within the culture of the organization. Untying from a stronghold culture of consensus threatens the loss of ownership.

CONSENSUS: THE TEMPTRESS OF CONFORMITY

"I'm not saying that everyone's opinions should be put into practice or every single complaint needs to be satisfied. That's what management judgment is all about. Obviously, some people have better ideas than others; some people are smarter or more experienced or more creative. But everyone should be heard and respected. They want it and you need it."

—JACK WELCH, *WINNING*

Distinguishing between consensus as a decision-making process and consensus as an objective or outcome is critical to judging its usefulness and effectiveness.

Here's what I mean. Consensus as a required outcome is not usually what's best for the organization because it promotes conformity without conviction. It urges arriving at a decision that is the least objectionable and the lowest common denominator, often defaulting to the status quo.

On the other hand, when consensus is viewed as a *process* versus an *outcome*, or a verb instead of a noun, it adds value to decision-making.

A genuine consensus decision-making process encourages *all* group members to openly share their unique perspectives, expertise, and any information they believe relevant to the discussion. When this is the case, decisions are better informed and commitment levels are greater.

Reaching a true consensus can be a complex process. It requires the genuine inclusion and active contribution of perspectives from all stakeholders. To work effectively, a consensus approach requires trust, active listening, and group participation.

To Sail With or Against the Current? That Is the Question...

"Most organizations prefer consensus and harmony over dissent and conflict."

—DANIEL KAHNEMAN, OLIVER SIBONY, AND CASS R. SUNSTEIN, *NOISE*

Group decision-making can be stressful, both for the group and for the leader. Think of a time when you were part of a group meeting where the objective was to agree on a decision. You've been there ... members of the group gathered around a table that both united and separated them.

Then there were members of the group peering down into the room from a screen on the wall, via a video connection. Maybe in total, there were eight group members, or maybe the group numbered fifteen or more.

As the discussion progresses, the faces on the wall move side to side as they scan the faces of the people around the table who are also *reading* their colleagues at table level, while intermittently referencing the faces of colleagues peering into the room. Everyone is taking mental notes and collecting signals to gauge the sentiment of the group. The captain is also looking for signals indicating the group's direction.

For consensus-driven captains, reaching agreement among the group is a condition of both organizational and personal success. Let's assume there are people with varying levels of status among the group. Most likely, the more senior people will be chomping at the bit to share their thoughts. The rest of the group, still collecting signals from their colleagues, are performing their own mental calculations. They are deciding whether they will hoist their "opinion sail," in which direction they will tack, or whether they will toe the line.

Conformity pressures loom large. As the discussion continues, the captain, proud of the intended "inclusive" discussion, stays focused on the ultimate prize: consensus. For the members of the group, the big knot that is tightening in their minds is becoming less about the actual issue at hand and more about the expected consensus outcome. Will they share information they may have that may go against the perceived tilt of the group, reveal their true position on the topic, echo and endorse what has already been said, or stay silent and ride the wave? This is a common group decision-making scenario, and it's an ideal opportunity for *conformity* to rule the room.

Even in this simple example, you can see why group decision-making is so complicated and often both exclusive and ineffective. Diversity of thought goes against the current, and going against the current involves risk to the unified spirit of the group. When consensus is treated as a goal, perspectives or opinions that don't align with the group current compromise a consensus outcome.

Research shows that more often than not, forced consensus results in bad decisions and poor outcomes due to two mind knots: conformity and groupthink.

The Constricting Cousins: Conformity and Groupthink

Conformity and groupthink are social biases that often work in tandem. They thrive in situations where there is a strong preference for or even an obsession with unity and consensus. And when group decision-making is unstructured and lacks a process to ensure freedom of thought and expression, these constricting mind knots are nearly certain to prevail.

Individual courage tends to get lost in group decision-making. These mental undercurrents help explain how even the best and brightest groups can fail in making good decisions. Sometimes groupthink can transform the most implausible ideas into perceived wisdom, making those who question them seem like outliers.

Conformity and groupthink constrict diversity of thought, strangling *inclusiveness*. Where groups engage in open dialogue that includes diversity of opinion, conflict, or logical debate, conformity will be challenged. Independent thinking and *expression* are the antidotes to groupthink.

Groupthink: A Prominent Organizational Knot

A decision endorsed by everyone in a group would appear to be an excellent outcome. Aren't more heads better than one? Not usually, as it turns out.

Cass Sunstein, Harvard Law School professor, co-author of *Wiser: Getting Beyond Groupthink to Make Groups Smarter,* and co-author of *Nudge,* revealed, "Group decisions increase conformity and decrease variance, without increasing accuracy." The extensive research examining groupthink conducted by Sunstein and co-author Reid Hastie affirmed that, while conformity unified decisions, it did not make them more accurate. Rather, conformity more often resulted in *wrong* decisions.

Group decision-making is a tricky proposition. As the research reveals, it often does more harm than good. Social psychologist Irving L. Janis coined the term "groupthink" in 1972, intending to explain the phenomenon in which people strive for consensus within a group.

Sometimes groupthink occurs as a result of direct pressure from others in the group who are concerned with maintaining cohesion and unity. The danger of groupthink is exemplified when "consensus" is tightly woven within the fabric of a company and culture. Good judgment and diversity of opinion are too often sacrificed for group cohesion. In some cases, people succumb to groupthink fearing their perspective or objection to the common thinking will affect the harmony of the pack. Group members may even hold back on sharing important information that would question the group's thinking.

And when a leader offers their perspective ahead of lower-ranking members of the group, groupthink is nearly certain.

Individuals may fear rejection by the group or leader, believing that raising a different perspective could consequently damage their inclusion within the team or even the company. The social identity of the group offers a comfortable sense of belonging among members, creating a vulnerable climate for groupthink to emerge.

Apparent consensus happens when individuals within the group stay away from controversy, avoiding any inclination to raise alternative considerations, thereby limiting the introduction of unique and independent thinking. Group loyalty often suppresses the sharing of individual perspectives, creating the illusion that group members are unified in their thinking, and therefore the decision must be correct. These dysfunctional dynamics significantly undermine the group's ability for sound reasoning and rational decision-making.

Volkswagen Unravels: Tragic Perils of Going with the Current

Consider a disastrous public example where the conformity bias impacted an entire company and its customers. For many years, the global automaker Volkswagen had been installing software in diesel cars to manipulate emissions tests and illegally sidestep pollution standards. In the face of clear dishonesty to its customers, Michael Horn, then head of Volkswagen Group of America, testified during a congressional hearing that he believed only "a couple of software engineers" were responsible. As many have pointed out, as of 2014, Volkswagen employed 583,000 people, and clearly the expansiveness of this installation would have required more than two people to be "in the know." And yet, there was silence.

Again, we can look to culture as a culprit. Volkswagen's culture has been described as being "brutally focused on achieving their goals." In his *Harvard Business Review* article, "High Cost of Conformity and How to Avoid It," Peter Bregman points out, "Seven years and 11 million cars later, you would think that someone would say something. But they did not. Why? Because saying something when nobody else is saying anything is really, really, hard."

Conforming is easier.

Catastrophic Challenger Mission

One of the most devastating examples of where conformity and groupthink biases led to tragedy was the *Challenger* launch in January 1986. Just seventy-three seconds after lift-off, the rocket transformed into a fiery explosion. This tragic event was found to have been caused by a malfunctioning joint and specifically, by the rubber O-ring component between two stages of the shuttle. It also became clear that in the months preceding the launch, engineers had raised safety issues related to the O-ring. NASA personnel, after discounting the engineers' concerns, persuaded them to reconsider. The engineers deliberated further and ultimately reversed their position. The announcement followed that the rocket was in good shape to fly. This tragedy could have been avoided.

In the interest of reducing conflict and striving for consensus, the engineers conformed. They did not consider alternatives. Morton Thiokol, the engineering company responsible for the solid rocket boosters, and NASA officials essentially ignored the expert opinion of the engineers and their concern about the O-ring issues and instead urged them to reconsider their position. This is a clear example of organizational dynamics and groupthink, and in this case, the group error resulted in the avoidable death of seven astronauts.

Strong leaders who are committed to the truth, and who can act with conviction, can find their way to taking the unpopular stand. In business organizations, most will not. Instead, many will choose to stay the course, avoiding disruption and sometimes the truth. Lacking the courage to express their position, many will instead go with the flow.

NAVIGATION KNOTS AND TACKS

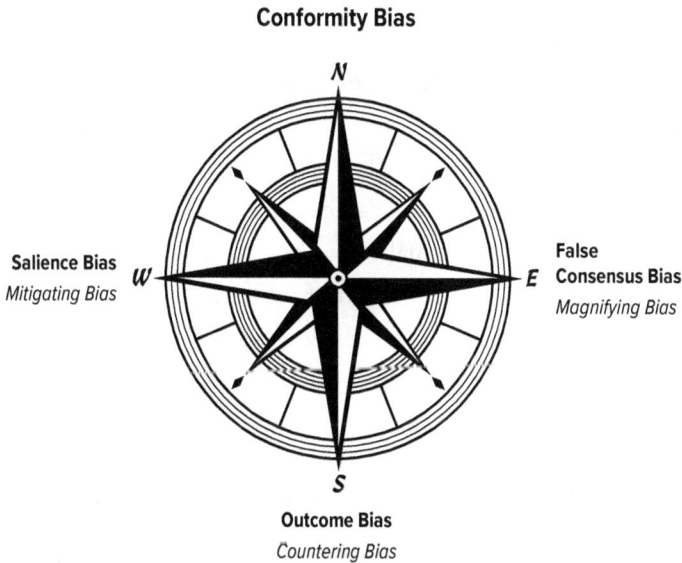

The Captain's Compass: Captains of All Hands and Minds

The primary mind knot in this chapter is conformity bias at the north cardinal point of the Captain's Compass. At the east cardinal point is false consensus bias, which amplifies errors of conformity.

Salience bias, at the west cardinal point, is a potential mitigating opportunity for these captains. At the south cardinal point is outcome bias, which offers a countering course for these leaders when combined with the courage of conviction and when the outcome on which they are focused is aligned with business objectives.

The North Cardinal Point: Conformity Bias

Conformity bias is the tendency to go along to get along. It causes individuals to conform to the crowd, even when they privately believe or know the crowd is wrong.

This bias causes leaders to make suboptimal decisions that could have serious consequences. In business, the pressure to conform can be overwhelming, whether deciding on a strategy, a capital investment, or new ways to do things. Conforming to group norms is often the easy thing to do to fit into an organization.

It's dangerous because it can cause leaders and teams to do things they wouldn't normally do. They can make poor decisions because they trust the judgment of others instead of their own. Or they may engage in risky behavior because everyone else is doing it. Leaders and businesses may also miss out on promising opportunities to avoid going against the current.

The East Cardinal Point: Magnifying Mind Knot
False Consensus Bias

When individuals overestimate the extent to which others agree with their views, they are influenced by false consensus bias.

This mind knot usually manifests in overconfidence and blindness to the actual reactions and opinions of others.

False consensus is an organizational obstruction. Conforming participants in the group can easily achieve a false consensus, despite the absence of critical thinking, evaluation, or honest discernment of individual viewpoints.

This mind knot is sometimes referred to as an "egocentric bias in social perception" because leaders in whom the bias is prevalent will completely ignore the possibility that others may have a different belief or opinion. Captains with this bias have a fundamental belief that their judgments are more prevalent than they actually are.

Tangled team dynamics and conformity-based thinking can create an echo-chamber effect, focusing decision-makers on a false *perception* of consensus, confirming their beliefs, and ultimately failing to account for potential risks associated with a *false* consensus.

The West Cardinal Point: Mitigating Mind Knot
The Salience Bias

Captains of All Hands and Minds can mitigate the course of conformity by adjusting their sail of saliency. Rather than projecting consensus as the important outcome objective in group decisions, these captains can leverage salience bias to clarify the *salient* business considerations and objectives in the decision process.

The psychological phenomenon of salience bias highlights the tendency to place more weight on that which is most pertinent to a decision. This mind knot has the power to sway how decision-makers perceive and interpret information by emphasizing the pertinence of a business objective, as opposed to defaulting to a consensus outcome, as the salient driving force in the decision-making process.

A word of caution. Salience bias can be influenced by emotions, beliefs, and past experiences, including a historical driving force such as consensus in group decision-making. In a culture that values tradition and the symbolism of a consensus outcome as prominent culture objectives, conformity and consistency will likely command attention as the salient purpose in decision-making.

Because our brain prefers the cognitive ease of making the choice that is easiest to digest, conformity and consensus are the least stressful options in this case. Therefore, to leverage the salience bias as a mitigating force to conformity and consensus, these captains must make clear the salient business objectives driving the decision-making process.

Salience bias can benefit these captains if they stay clear-eyed, setting the group's sights on aligning decisions with business priorities and goals as outcome objectives. Then these captains can redirect the emotionally motivated reasoning of the group from a preferred consensus outcome to a more salient and worthy decision that is aligned with the goals of the business.

Captains of All Hands and Minds can steer away from a symbolic construct of coherence and consensus to the critical business objectives of the company by leveraging the salience bias.

The South Cardinal Point: Countering Mind Knot

The Outcome Bias

The Outcome Bias encourages leaders to make a decision based on a desired outcome rather than focusing on the considerations of getting to the outcome.

Good decision-making should be judged on the integrity of the decision process and not on the quality of the outcome of the decision. On the surface, an outcome bias influence would work against this principle. However, as a counter to conformity and consensus decision-making, this bias can be useful.

Outcome bias can encourage independent thinking when decisions are outcome focused. By emphasizing that decisions are focused on a specific business objective or outcome and not based on group consensus as an outcome, these leaders can set the stage for independent and critical thinking throughout the decision process.

A focus on a business outcome highlights that the quality of the decision is based on the quality of the decision *process*, and not on how popular or widely accepted the decision is. If individuals understand they may be judged on the outcome of the decision, instead of a symbolic consensus outcome, they may feel a heightened sense of responsibility for their contribution to the decision process.

When these captains focus on the importance of the decision tied to a business outcome, this bias can serve as an effective counter to conformity, groupthink and consensus.

A properly directed outcome bias offers an easing away from conformity and toward business-directed judgment grounded in a sound process including cognitive diversity, decisiveness, and conviction for decisions that align with clear business objectives.

NAVIGATING THE CONFORMITY BIAS

Questions: Know Your Knots

- Am I striking a balance between respecting group consensus and relying on my independent judgment when making a decision?
- Do I recognize the influence of group dynamics and social pressure on my decisions, and am I vigilant about avoiding conformity bias in my organization?
- Do I trust my own judgment and critical thinking skills when evaluating decisions, or am I overly swayed by the opinions of others?

Tacking Techniques

- Focus on business objectives instead of an idealistically driven consensus outcome.
- Ensure information and discussions are focused on salient business considerations throughout the decision process.
- Follow a sound and structured decision process for information- and opinion-gathering. Leaders speak last to avoid authority influence and give everyone the opportunity to share information, ideas, and opinions.
- Get the right crew members involved—consider expertise over rank.
- Focus on the process and not the win with a pre-meeting strategy—the McKinsey way. Share key information, data, and messaging with stakeholders in advance of the meeting, setting in motion the process of alignment and buy-in. The pre-meeting process provides the opportunity

to understand the dynamics and perspectives of individual stakeholders, positive and negative. Identifying detractors and concerns in advance of the meeting provides the runway to address concerns in advance of the meeting, enabling genuine consensus on the issue, deterring false consensus due to conformity and groupthink.

- Collect uncensored individual opinions and relevant data, in person or in writing, ahead of the meeting to ensure every member is given an equal voice and to avoid "going along to get along" during the meeting.
- Pay attention to the *current* of the group, and designate members as "logic testers" and conformity challengers.

THE RATIONAL SOLUTION

The question is, how do Captains of All Hands and Minds draw upon their conformity bias to leverage it as an advantage in decision-making, while leading with conviction toward a good outcome?

Outcome and Conviction: The Transformers of Conformity

"Only the leader can set the tone of the dialogue in the organization. Dialogue is the core of culture and the basic unit of work. How people talk to each other absolutely determines how well the organization will function."

—LARRY BOSSIDY AND RAM CHARAN,
EXECUTION: THE DISCIPLINE OF GETTING THINGS DONE

In 2011, when Larry Page assumed the CEO role at Google, he almost immediately upended the consensus culture that was shaping the company's modus operandi. In fact, Page insisted that a decision-maker be present in every meeting, and if that were not the case, the meeting should not happen. He understood that an enormous cost of consensus was speed. Perhaps he also fell into the camp of other leaders who believe a consensus approach is often a proxy for procrastination, whether intentional or not. Page asserted and believed, "There are no companies that make good slow decisions."

Jeff Bezos, founder of Amazon, also openly cautioned against the danger of consensus in a letter to his shareholders in 2016. He directly encouraged his team to avoid chasing agreement and instead acknowledge disagreement and act with conviction. He asked them to "gamble with him."

The way Bezos saw it, teams should have enough trust in each other that they do not require total agreement to commit. "Disagree and commit" was the Bezos mantra. Conformity for the sake of consensus in decision-making has no place in the Amazon environment.

Bezos is an example of a visionary leader who leveraged the virtue of conformity in terms of driving consensus *around vision, purpose, and business outcome*, while boldly acting with conviction against the norm to create a global business and a successful outsized model of commerce.

Conviction is predicated on a measure of belief and the consistent construction of a goal, versus the random choices of the moment. Therefore, where these captains can adjust their thinking from a framework tied to consensus, or collective thinking, toward decisiveness based on conviction, they will be better positioned to avoid the pitfalls of conformity and groupthink.

Conviction and decisiveness matter in leadership. A *Harvard Business Review* article published in 2017, "What Sets Successful CEOs Apart," identifies conviction in decision-making as one of the four key behaviors distinguishing exceptional CEOs from the rest. Authors Botelho, Powell, Kincaid, and Wang note, "We discovered that high-performing CEOs do not necessarily stand out for making great decisions all the time; rather, they stand out for being more decisive. They made decisions earlier, faster, and with greater conviction."

Harmonizing

"You don't get harmony when everybody sings the same note."

—DOUG FLOYD

Nonconformists think outside the box. They diverge from common thinking, which opens the door for both innovation and risk. Nonconformity is often a sign of confidence, creative thinking, and deliberate and honest intentionality, though when consensus is the outcome mandate, conformity and groupthink tend to rule the decision.

Organizations led by captains with conviction are the antithesis of consensus-driven leaders.

Steve Jobs was a nonconformist and a consensus leader at the same time. He was a pioneer of "thinking different," though simultaneously, he critically drove consensus around the Apple vision. Jobs insisted his leaders intently articulate his vision for Apple, ensuring all employees understood it clearly, felt deep purpose in carrying it out, and acted in sync with the company's vision. He created a culture of consensus when it came to the purpose of the company, while at the same time, he empowered people to think differently, applying their individual creativity decisively and with conviction, though in alignment to the Apple vision and company objectives.

Jobs also found a way to leverage consensus in resolving conflict. He followed what he described as a diplomatic approach. He would bring people together to talk through the issue until an agreement was reached. And when it came to the most critical decisions for the company, he relied on his policy team made up of eight people. Jobs stated, "For the really important decisions, we work on it until we all agree."

Practical Conformity, Personal Accountability, and Conviction

Tony Hseih, the former CEO of Zappos, and referred to by some as a brilliant eccentric, instituted a "common consent" model known as holacracy, which governed the ways of working at Zappos. This model made the company a total collective operating environment focused on conformity to the "organization of work instead of the organization of people," forging small "circles of accountability" across the entire company.

This holacratic model required "internalization," the most penetrating of the three varieties of conformity referenced earlier. In this case, conforming and committing to the model raised the bar from a consensus-driven culture. Where a true consensus culture aims to have people feel included in decision-making, and ultimately to buy into an agreed decision, a holacratic model creates a highly participative and contributing work environment where every voice has value and can act with conviction to make an impact.

Far from conventional organizational structures, and even those more insightful organizations just mentioned, Captain Hsieh took perhaps the most extreme view of blending conformity with outcome through conviction. His model deliberately focused on strengthening the company's connected and unified culture and focus on customers, while fostering conscientiousness, individual initiative, and accountability. His move to a holacratic system wove empowerment into the culture and fabric of the organization. Similar to, though more extreme than, the models Page, Bezos, and Jobs employed, Hsieh's model also leveraged both conformity and conviction to achieve the organization's goals.

At the time of his death, Captain Hsieh was five years into transitioning Zappos to the model of holacracy. Brian Robertson, the founder of holacracy, makes clear the problem with consensus. "By trying to reach consensus, we're shifting the focus from one person who senses one tension to a group process. The trouble with that is that the 'group' isn't the ultimate sensing instrument – I am, and you are." Robertson's point is that it is the individuals close to the tension, issue, or decision who are in the best position to act decisively and with conviction to address the reality of the organizational issue.

The focus of a horizontal, holacratic culture is the efficiency of work. Instead of leaders having authority over teams and people, as in a traditional hierarchical organization, in a holacracy model it is the role, not the person, that holds the authority. It is a form of self-management where decision-making power is conferred on work circles or fluid teams and roles instead of on individuals. And it only works when the entire organization is committed and *conforms* to its tenets, philosophy, and ways of working.

The theory behind holacracy is that it provides flexibility and the uniqueness of each person's talents to emerge and be voiced and expressed at the operational level. In contrast, heavily matrixed structures and complex reporting relationships surrounding teams typically get in the way of exposing perspectives and diverse thinking, thereby thwarting team effectiveness and productivity.

This structure removes the illusion of consensus through a process that captures the authentic voice of everyone, while also harnessing the sentiment of the stakeholder group. Leadership decisions are counterbalanced by individual and group expression. The integrity of decision-making is measured against the organization's goals and mission. The bar is set higher than in a consensus-driven culture, because it focuses on the organization of work and not people, thus eliminating power plays, personal agendas, and group sway.

The essence of holacracy is that it inherently strips away the risk of any one powerful individual directing or swaying the thinking or activities of others. The system aims to provide greater reliability and adaptability for the organization. It is critically dependent on all individuals conforming to its philosophy and ways of working, while at the same time it relies on individual voices, their power, decisiveness, and conviction in decision-making.

The "Purpose" Driver of Conformity, Outcome, and Conviction

Page, Bezos, Jobs, and Hsieh all understood the power of conformity and its significance for company purpose and values. They also understood it was the interplay of purpose-based conformity and conviction that would propel their leadership and companies to greatness. Each of these leaders had this natural insight, and each in their own way operated within the framework of an "Inclusive Outcome Model." Common and core to each of their leadership and culture models was *purpose* and doing what is right for the organization. These were the enablers to effectively combine the merits of conformity with decisiveness and conviction in order to achieve progressive movement, momentum, and significant outcomes.

Purpose reflects an organization's reason for being. It outlasts and outperforms any one business outcome direction. Purpose encompasses the essence, spirit, and aligned values around what the organization is genuinely aiming to accomplish.

Start with Why, written by Simon Sinek, highlights the concept of operating toward the core purpose, cause, and mission of the business. Not from the standpoint of *how* an organization operates or what it does, but rather, *why* the organization does what it does or makes the important decisions it makes. When conformity to purpose is combined with an appropriately directed outcome bias, both inclusive decisions and business outcomes can prevail.

Focusing on the "why" guides thinking and decision-making beyond the activities of a business to the alignment of those activities to the organization's purpose, mission, objectives, and outcome strategy.

The Inclusive Outcome Model: The Way Forward

An organization's competitive advantage are its people and decision-making, which affects execution, speed, innovation, and outcomes. When decision processes and models are flawed, execution and outcomes fail.

The Inclusive Outcome Model does not work to the exclusion of either conformity or consensus. Rather it factors in critical thinking, discernment, and the leader's conviction, while at the same time considering the inclusive voices and sentiments of the stakeholder group. It aims to treat consensus as an approach to a decision, not as an outcome in and of itself.

Consensus is more often a proxy for the median. Outcome ownership and conviction are a measure of decisiveness based on the "best" ideas. When a decision process is genuinely *inclusive*, it becomes a catalyst opportunity and not an optical illusion of consensus.

Conviction is preceded by consideration and sensitivity to distributed thinking—thinking away from the norm, the ordinary, and the status quo. It paves the way for value creation.

Therefore, there are two critical elements conforming to the organization's purpose and goals, and with conviction, making the best decision for the organization, even where there may not be consensus. Leaders then become facilitators of inclusion for the value of diversity of thought, lifting individuals, teams, and enterprises.

This mixed mental approach can be achieved by applying the concept I've named the Inclusive Outcome Model. It separates Captains of All Hands and Minds who have the mental agility to blend conformity and outcome bias from *consensus-bound* captains who fall prey to conformity and groupthink. The model facilitates leaders and organizations to commit to *conformity to purpose*, enabling decisiveness and conviction to achieve organizational objectives and outcomes.

THE BOTTOM LINE: ALL HANDS ON DECK

"A leader is one who knows the way, goes the way, and shows the way."

—JOHN C. MAXWELL

Inclusive Outcome Mission Objectives

· Strengthen the integrity of organizational decision-making, avoiding "common thinking," groupthink, and false consensus.
· Honor consensus as a process versus an outcome.
· Leverage the power of conformity toward commitment to purpose, strategy, mission, and values, in combination with conviction and decisiveness focused on organizational objectives and outcomes.

The Strategy Equation

Conformity Bias + Outcome Bias =
The Inclusive Outcome Model

Establishing a culture of open communication, critical thinking, and collaboration is key to overcoming conformity bias. Challenging the status quo and encouraging the team to openly express dissenting views is the mandate for these leaders. It is critically important for these captains to be aware of potential pressures that can lead to conformity bias and groupthink, including organizational culture, power dynamics, and deadlines.

Charts a new course steering conforming and consensus-driven captains into inclusive and decisive leaders.

Strategic Maneuvers and Organizational Guidance: The Inclusive Outcome Model

The Captain

- Keep a decision journal to record your thought processes, assumptions, and reasons behind your decisions. Audit for conformity, groupthink, and false consensus bias insights.
- Review past decisions, where conformity bias may have played a role. Analyze the decision-making process and its outcomes to identify areas to improve the decision process.
- Develop protocols that prevent "common thinking" and least-common-denominator decisions, and instead promote discernment, conviction, and rational decision-making.

- Encourage "rocking the boat" to avoid the sway of conformity.
- Adopt a system of checks and balances where decisions are made objectively without the influence of any single individual or group. Ensure team members have enough time to reflect on decisions, ask questions, and share ideas before finalizing them.

The Crew—Leadership Team

- Form groups based on expertise and not rank.
- Encourage diverse perspectives and dissenting opinions by providing opportunities for team members to express their ideas and concerns privately. Recognize those who offer unconventional ideas.
- Assign a devil's advocate or critic within the decision group who has the courage to provide honest feedback, someone who can spot the *current* of conformity and who can draw out dissenting perspectives, the enemy of groupthink.
- Leverage retrospectives to identify and address conformity and groupthink tendencies in group dynamics. Test the logic of a decision once the decision is made.
- Implement regular decision audits or reviews where decisions are examined for conformity and conspiring biases.

People Processes

- Integrate training programs on groupthink and conformity bias into leadership development and employee training programs. Explain the value of conforming to vision, purpose, mission, and outcomes. Highlight risk associated with conformity and groupthink. Provide tools for recognizing and mitigating these biases.

- Assess for conformity bias as part of the candidate due diligence and selection process. Look for evidence of appreciation for others, balanced thinking, decisiveness, and goal orientation.

Financial Considerations

- Encourage finance teams to consider a variety of financial models and scenarios, even if they challenge conventional thinking.
- Leverage data-driven processes to reduce the influence of conformity in financial forecasting.
- Track the financial impact of decisions and outcomes linked to conformity, groupthink, or consensus-based decisions.

Commercial Considerations

- Prioritize market research and customer feedback processes that involve external perspectives, reducing the influence of internal groupthink on commercial decisions.

Board Considerations

- Promote diversity within the board to ensure a broad range of perspectives and to reduce the risk of conformity bias.
- Hold the captain accountable for a culture of conformity to the organization's purpose and mission rather than a culture of consensus.

- Encourage board members to actively seek external perspectives and industry insights to counter conformity and groupthink.

Five Questions to Identify Indicators of Conformity Bias

1. What is your approach to ensuring that the voices of all key decision stakeholders are heard and considered ahead of making a final decision?
2. How often do you reassess prior decisions and consider new evidence or data?
3. Are you open to feedback from your team, even if it is not in line with what you initially believed?
4. When presented with a new idea that strays from popular thinking of the group, do you consider it objectively or immediately reject it?
5. How do you handle a situation where the entire group follows suit in an argument supporting a decision? Do you seek out alternative strategies and solutions when faced with this challenge, or do you accept the common thinking of the group as the best solution, even when you believe otherwise?

TAKEAWAYS: TYING IT ALL TOGETHER

Captains of All Hands and Minds

These captains are facilitators of conformity, often promoters of consensus as a targeted outcome, at the expense of the actual business outcome to which they are driving. Their opportunity is to treat consensus as an effective approach to a decision-making process rather than the goal of the decision.

It is their strong penchant for unity that creates the space for conformity and groupthink, resulting in ineffective information processing and suboptimal decisions. Bound to consensus, common thinking prevails, leading to mediocre or suboptimal outcomes.

Conformity Bias

Conformity bias urges people to fall in line with group norms and guidance, believing others know better than they do. Oftentimes, team members will choose to conform either explicitly or by omission to avoid rocking the boat for their team or the organization.

This mind knot draws others into common thinking, anchoring teams and organizations to the status quo, preventing good decisions that could move the organization forward or even save it from a crisis situation.

The Rational Solution: The Inclusive Outcome Model

This model values and honors conformity to organizational vision, purpose, and outcomes, superseding an outcome emphasis on conformity and consensus. The framework provides actionable suggestions aimed at reducing errors due to conformity bias while promoting an inclusive decision process focused on salient business objectives.

SIX

THE OPTIMISM BIAS

"A pessimist sees the difficulty in every opportunity; an optimist sees the opportunity in every difficulty."
—WINSTON CHURCHILL

THE OPTIMISM BIAS

D O YOU SEE THE GLASS AS HALF EMPTY OR HALF FULL? The glass and its contents are constant, while your answer to that question reveals your attitudes and perceptions.

The lens through which we view the world matters. And it absolutely matters in leadership.

Optimism bias guides our perception through a filter of positivity, urging us to believe that good things are more likely to happen than bad things. This mental shortcut urges optimistic leaders to overestimate the likelihood of expected positive outcomes, and to underestimate the results of risky decisions and the probability of negative outcomes. Optimism bias produces an *overly* optimistic outlook, even when evidence suggests otherwise.

The phenomenon of optimism is attributed to psychological factors including wishful thinking and the tendency to focus on positive thoughts rather than unpleasant ones. Rational thinking doesn't always factor into decision-making when optimism bias is at the helm; instead, emotion often takes precedence.

CAPTAINS OF SAILS

Captains of Sails are optimists who view the future as the opportunity to create their destiny. They will almost always view the glass as half full.

With winds of optimism at their back, these leaders sail away from the status quo in the pursuit of lofty aspirations and possibilities. Captains of Sails give everything a positive twist, finding they can rationalize just about anything. And they do.

These captains are influencers with strong interpersonal and relationship-nurturing skills. Trusting, contactable, self-confident, and enthusiastically persuasive, Captains of Sails inspire others. They promote new ideas and products. They inspire visions of hope and tend to make emotionally based decisions.

With an ability to read verbal and nonverbal cues, these leaders often have a sixth sense about their customers' needs and wants. With sense and skill, they build incredible relationships and help their customers achieve their dreams.

Optimism can be one of the greatest strengths of these leaders, making them confident and resilient.

But optimism bias also produces blind spots when it comes to risk, causing distortions in mental processing—twisted judgment, tangled decision-making, and even reckless choices. Unbridled optimism creates a wide array of problems. It can cause leaders to ignore risk warning signals or to doubt expert advice, leading to costly mistakes. On a macro level, for instance, excessive optimism can prevent organizations from adapting quickly enough in the face of changing conditions.

At its core, this psychological bias is a product of emotion rather than reason, which makes understanding it even more important for leaders.

Let's take a deeper look into the blessing and curse of optimism for Captains of Sails.

The Optimism Mind Knot and Captains of Sails

Optimism is a powerful force that can have a profound impact on decision-making, leadership, and the overall success of a business.

It inspires motivation, confidence, and perseverance to tackle the toughest of challenges, generating innovative solutions that can transform businesses.

For Captains of Sails who are motivated by the ability to control their destiny and to achieve their dreams, optimism is never far from the helm. Envisioning a future that improves the status quo, these captains will fiercely pursue outcomes that are bigger and better than most can imagine. They invite others into the dream—nurturing hope and creating anticipation of a better product, a better service, and a better future. They are extremely effective at stirring emotion and creating exciting expectations.

The "glass-half-full" perspective of optimism is often a life-boat for these leaders, keeping them afloat or alive long enough to fight through the next storm or to win the next victory. Even in the toughest of storms, it provides an important means of sustenance in the pursuit of dreams and goals.

You might be asking: what's wrong with seeing the glass half full or focusing on a positive future? Don't we want our captains to lead us to our dream destination? The answer is, of course, yes. It's no secret that optimism can be a powerful tool in leadership. But what happens when optimism goes too far?

While the upside of optimism does indeed have a glow to it, the problem is that the glow can be blinding, causing these captains to venture into risky waters unprepared. A step too far can be detrimental because it hijacks a leader's mind, creating the potential for failure. Optimism can drive leaders into a state of blind confidence, distracting them from important information and causing them to overestimate their ability to control outcomes.

And when other biases that move in a direction similar to optimism are also in play, well, potential consequences become even graver.

Optimism Colluders and Kinks

At this point in the book it should be clear that we seldom see one mind knot without another. There are natural relationships among different biases that can cause multiple kinks and knots in our thinking, compounding bad decisions.

For instance, there is a natural codependency between the optimism and overconfidence biases. This common double mind knot ties these biases together, and the negative effect of each bias is strengthened by the other.

Overconfidence bias conspiring with optimism bias convinces Captains of Sails that they *will* achieve their goals. Overestimating their capabilities, they will forge ahead with a false sense of confidence.

Things get even worse when a third colluding bias is braided in: the illusion of control. This mind knot further seduces and tangles the optimistic and overconfident minds of these captains, convincing them they have both the capability and ultimate control over their journey.

Sometimes this "triple knot" of optimism, overconfidence, and an illusion of control can fuel the momentum necessary to achieve a desired outcome. It *can* be used as a compound force for good when these biases are managed. Other times, it can spell disaster, causing Captains of Sails to dismiss threats and risks until they find themselves completely in over their heads. They are prone to sailing into troubled waters without counting the cost.

For better or worse, they are Captains of Sails.

The Upside of Optimism in Sales

"Twenty years from now, you will be more disappointed by the things you didn't do than by the things you did. So, throw off the bowlines. Sail away from the harbor. Catch the trade winds in your sails."

—MARK TWAIN

One reason Captains of Sails may leave their optimism mind knot unaddressed is that it has probably worked well for them in the past. For instance, research shows that outcomes of optimistic sales professionals far exceed outcomes of non-optimistic salespeople. The studies also show that optimistic sales professionals handle rejection better than others, enabling them to persist in moving forward.

Dr. Martin Seligman, the father of positive psychology, conducted research on the impact of optimism in sales. In the mid-1980s, he was approached by the CEO of MetLife and asked to test for optimism in the company's hiring process.

The insurance company typically hired 5,000 sales consultants a year and invested nearly $150 million in training every two years to ensure success. They also had all recruits take a sales aptitude test as part of the hiring process. The outcome? Half of the recruits quit within their first year, and there was an 80 percent turnover rate across the remaining sales force every four years.

Dr. Seligman introduced his "optimism test" into the MetLife sales hiring process, and the results were remarkable. In a study group where *all* consultants had passed the sales aptitude test, optimists outperformed pessimists by 8 percent in year one. By year two, the optimists were outselling the pessimists by a whopping 31 percent.

This contrast was even starker among consultants who *didn't* pass the sales aptitude test. Super optimists in this group outsold the pessimists in the group by 21 percent in year one and 57 percent in year two.

This was an astounding revelation. The correlation between optimism and sales success outweighed the correlation between sales aptitude and sales success.

Seligman's results were consistent when tested across different industries. Optimistic salespeople outperformed their pessimistic colleagues anywhere from 20 to 40 percent.

Why is this?

Dr. Seligman concluded that optimists do not perceive failure as inherent. They view it as an obstacle they can overcome. Taking accountability for their own success is the captain's first step in using this bias for good.

Oceans of Consequence

"What I've really learned over time is that optimism is a very, very important part of leadership."
—BOB IGER, FORMER CHAIRMAN AND CEO,
WALT DISNEY COMPANY

Captains of Sails depend on others. They sail for their company, stakeholders, and customers. These captains are in the business of making dreams come true.

Tom Watson Sr., the founder of International Business Machines (IBM), believed that "real sailors" were developed on rough seas. He instituted professional sales across the IBM enterprise and set the standard for well-educated salespeople. As a result, IBM produced a highly trained, optimistic, and motivated sales force, which enabled the company to pull ahead of its competitors.

Competitive CEOs like Watson know that the time to prepare and plan is well before the sail. There is no time for studying or crafting the plan once in the clutches of a volatile business ocean.

And here's where the Captains of Sails can struggle. Blinded by optimism and overconfidence and focused on the positive future ahead, they may fail to recognize that bad things can happen. They sail forward, propelled by emotion, without giving adequate thought to how to effectively navigate challenges.

Peter Isler, a famous sailing champion and business advisor, writes, "How a sailor reacts to a change in conditions is what sets a good sailor apart from others....In business, leaders need to think on their feet to survive....Simply being optimistic and relying on what has been tried and tested in business is not enough."

At sea and in business, staying still is not an option. The world of business requires preparation as well as continually navigating constant waves to maintain a competitive advantage. Sometimes captains win, and sometimes captains lose.

But two things are certain: the waves and decisions of the business ocean always have consequences for everyone involved. And to survive, these Captains of Sails must retain their optimism while understanding how to navigate ever-changing threats.

Dream Pursuers

Captains of Sails are their own destiny-makers. Optimistically charting their course to satisfy their need for freedom and independence, these leaders seek responsibility and accept the risk of the sail. They go all-in on their dreams, which is often physically and mentally draining.

They sail with purpose, envisioning an improved future. Yet these dreams often require more than just optimism. And sometimes optimism clouds reality enough to hinder their dreams.

When turbulence strikes, these leaders are forced to accept that their ability to control their ocean is indeed an optimistic illusion.

Dreams Devoured by the Sea

On September 20, 1991, the *Andrea Gail* departed from Gloucester Harbor, Massachusetts. With Captain Billy Tyne at the helm, the 72-foot commercial fishing vessel was headed to the swordfish-rich waters of the Grand Banks of Newfoundland, 900 miles away. For the optimistic and fearless Captain Tyne, the fish represented both his dream and his fortune.

Tyne was regarded as one of the most successful captains in the commercial swordfish business. Even though the timing of his sail meant that he and his crew would be facing treacherous fall seas, he decided to press on. His optimistic dream of fish holds filled to the brim overshadowed the looming risk of serious seasonal storms. His optimism was infectious, and any initial reservations of the crew were quickly allayed as they sailed into the calm waters of the Atlantic.

Captain Tyne made the brazen choice to navigate further out than originally planned, to the Flemish Cap. There the *Andrea Gail* found herself in seas that were swarming with swordfish. The crew tirelessly hauled and packed the fish with ice until the holds were nearly full. With 40,000 pounds of dreams on board, the boat's ice machine began to falter—forcing Tyne to head back to Gloucester, before their dreams were spoiled.

Underway, it became certain they would encounter a serious fight against an escalating storm. Confident they could control the *Andrea Gail* and handle whatever came their way, the captain and crew proceeded into the storm to keep their dreams alive.

What they didn't fully understand is that they were about to head into what is now referred to as "The Storm of the Century."

With unwavering determination to deliver their dream catch, both captain and crew succumbed to the triple knot of optimism, overconfidence, and the illusion of control.

The storm was an anomaly of historic proportions, with waves up to 100 feet. Though they were optimistic, the intensity of the storm they encountered was far beyond what they could ever control.

Tragically, the storm claimed the lives of all six crew members. The *Andrea Gail* has never been found.

Optimism can capture dreams, breed success, and fill sails. Mismanaged optimism can send captains and their crew into deep and dark waters.

Plight of the Pitch

In nautical terms, pitch refers to the up-and-down movement of a boat in response to the motion of the ocean. Captains of Sails must masterfully adjust their sales "pitch" in response to the motion of their "sea"—their markets and their customers.

In sales, pitching provides the opportunity for these captains to skillfully demonstrate their ability to move to the rhythm of their sea of customers. When their pitch is in sync with their sea, they achieve momentum.

Optimism affects the pitch. Sometimes it urges these captains to do too little pitching, and sometimes too much pitching. Other times, their pitch can be completely off course, ultimately plunging them into a wave of chaos.

However, captains who skillfully leverage their optimism to positively frame their pitch in alignment with their customers can create the movement necessary to gain momentum.

The Framing Effect is a cognitive bias that influences choices based on the way they are framed and pitched. People are more likely to make a choice that is framed in an appealing way. Framing decorates and draws focus to the dream. As fearless dreamers, Captains of Sails will often find the framing effect to be an effective pitching strategy for their sail.

These captains can use framing and their interpersonal skills to leverage their optimism for good, adapting their pitch to the changing seas of their customers.

Optimism, Relationships, and Momentum

There are three key relationships for Captains of Sails: their sea (customers), their organization (boat), and their crew. Let's examine how optimism is the key to the power and interconnectedness of these relationships and how captains can use this power to build organizational momentum.

Optimism and the Sea: Relationships to Customers and Markets
Captains of Sails survive and thrive on positive relationships with their customers and their markets—understanding the sea in which they sail can never be overlooked or underappreciated.

Optimism invigorates these leaders, giving them the determination to pursue and nurture relationships. These relationships become critical to creating movement and gaining momentum.

The challenge they face is not to allow their optimism to dismiss or ignore changes affecting key customer relationships or changes in market conditions. They must temper their optimism with honesty and reality to keep effectively adjusting their pitch and framing.

Optimism and the Boat: The Captain's Organization

Organizations are the vessels through which Captains of Sails deliver customer dreams.

Sailor and businessman John Kretschmer advises, "Find the positive and work to leverage it...Use your *boat's* best assets." He challenges every captain to ask the question, "Can you forereach [gain on another vessel] when you need to?"

If Captains of Sails are not optimistic about the seaworthiness of their boat, the sail is compromised. In addition to optimism, the boat must also be in objectively good condition and well-equipped for a proper sail. If the boat isn't sound, it creates drag that will seriously compromise potential. If the boat doesn't have the capability to forereach, there can be no movement, and no momentum.

Optimism and the Crew

"The crew matters too," writes Kretschmer. "Having a talented helmsman is critical. But just as importantly, having someone who maintains optimism as the weather deteriorates is a tremendous asset on any boat."

Here again we see the complicated and important relationship between optimism and competence.

Optimism is a key component in the relationships captains build with customers, their organization, and their crew. It is an invaluable asset when managed, mobilized, and monitored.

The Captain with Dangerous Dreams

"If it feels like you're choosing between the lesser of two evils, don't. There is always a higher choice."

—MICHAEL NEILL, AUTHOR, SPEAKER, COACH

Captain Billy Tyne was an honorable and highly respected captain who made a tragic miscalculation. This next story is one of a very different sort of captain—one who was dishonorable and tragically blinded by the very dark side of optimism bias.

It began in 1966, when Sir Francis Chichester single-handedly voyaged around the globe in his custom-built *Gipsy Moth IV*—a 53-foot ketch sailboat. Intent on racing against records set in the 19th century by clipper ships, 64-year-old Chichester optimistically took the helm, had a victorious sail, and created a worldwide stir.

The Sunday Times covered Chichester's voyage, and in 1968 the paper created a new challenge: the Golden Globe Race. They successfully summoned nine optimistic captains to try to recreate Chichester's solo voyage.

The *Times* did not evaluate the sailing ability of their recruits and there were few to no rules governing the race, except for the requirement to set sail, alone, between June 1 and October 31.

Of the nine captains who competed, only one finished— Robin Knox-Johnston and his ketch-rigged double-ended yacht *Suhaili*. Seven other captains quit the race.

The ninth, Donald Crowhurst, was the last captain to set sail, and it is his story that is perhaps most illustrative of the destructive force of optimism, overconfidence, and the illusion of control.

A business entrepreneur and weekend sailor, Crowhurst embraced the opportunity to enter the race while showcasing his invention, the Navicator, a handheld direction finder designed to identify marine and aviation beacons. (Remember, this was 1968, long before computers and GPS.) He thought that a successful race with his invention could help him gain notoriety, prize money, and long-term security for his family.

Described by others as having a "dominating and supercharged personality," Crowhurst yearned for the world stage. The Golden Globe Race was his dream opportunity.

Crowhurst was also reportedly overly secure in his intelligence, charm, and skills. Many reported, "He had an extraordinary ability to get people to believe him." His positive framing and pitching enabled him to attract prominent investors in his sail. He also mortgaged his business and home to help fund the building of his boat, exposing himself and his family to serious financial risk. And as the cherry on top, he hired a publicist to showcase his story.

Crazily confident in the "probable" performance of his custom-built trimaran boat, Crowhurst was convinced he would win the fastest voyage award, despite being the last of the captains to set sail.

He minimized critical risk factors, including the unproven success of trimarans as vessels for voyaging around the world. These boats have a lack of stability, speed, and seaworthiness in angry waves. Also, the only time Crowhurst had ever sailed this type of vessel was a couple of weeks prior when he had taken the delivery of his unfinished boat.

Delaying his departure until the last possible day, he set sail with multiple unfinished "innovative" features. He planned to take care of any outstanding issues once underway. But wrapped up in the emotion of setting sail, he mistakenly headed out to sea without the supplies and parts necessary for these "on-the-job" repairs.

Crowhurst soon realized his actual sailing speed was only half the pace of his optimistic projections. Circling in the Atlantic Ocean, he considered he might only have a 50 percent chance of surviving the Southern Ocean if he was not able to complete the unfinished safety features on his boat. Ultimately, he realized his boat could not survive the voyage ahead.

The captain reviewed his options: quitting the race, which would result in near financial collapse and personal humiliation or continuing in his unseaworthy boat and facing near certain death.

Crowhurst's hubris steered him toward a third option. He schemed to hide out in the South Atlantic Ocean for months. He let his competitors circumnavigate the globe while he falsified his navigation logs to reflect that he too braved and prevailed against the monstrous Southern Seas.

He planned to sail back at just the right time and intentionally finish last to avoid scrutinization of his navigational logs.

Unexpectedly, Robin Knox-Johnston completed the race. But all the other sailors were out. Because he was last to sail, Crowhurst's false reports actually put him in a position where he was expected to be the fastest finisher.

Crowhurst's dishonesty was compounded with increasing boasts of his positioning as being "off Cape Town." Then, a misunderstood transmission from his faltering radio created the illusion he was speedily advancing to the finish.

Press coverage, along with an organized reception of boats, helicopters, and British welcomers, were all in motion in anticipation of his forthcoming arrival. Captain Crowhurst soon realized he could not possibly fulfill the false expectations he set for himself.

By June 29, Crowhurst ended all radio communication. He entered his last logbook entry on July 1. On July 10, 1969, his boat was found adrift...absent its captain. It is assumed Crowhurst made the fatal choice to plunge into the deep blue sea.

This captain abandoned his integrity and could not sustain the sail. All the optimism, overconfidence, and illusions of control in the world could not deliver his dream. In fact, this triple mind knot ultimately destroyed both the dream and the man.

Captains of Sails often have to make decisions between less than ideal options—whether in negotiating terms of a deal, choosing the right direction in which to move the mission forward, or even whether to abandon it altogether. These choices require good judgment and never losing sight of their critical relationships. Managing optimism while making these choices requires awareness, honesty, and integrity. It is the only way forward.

Illusion of Control and Selective Perception

In anticipation of winning, these two captains—one honorable, one dishonorable—fell prey to both the illusion of control and selective perception mind knots. Selective perception causes us to miss or dismiss signals that either contradict our vision or make us emotionally uncomfortable. This bias influences us to interpret information in a way that is aligned with our existing beliefs.

The illusion of control and selective perception create false frameworks that keep these captains forging forward, even in situations when forward is the poor choice.

Captain Marty: Optimism Sinks the Bottom Line

During a client engagement, I had the opportunity to work with a proud sales captain, we'll call him Marty, who led the commercial business for the largest division within a multi-billion-dollar global company. It was well known across the company that Captain Marty and his crew were onboarding impressive numbers. In fact, Marty was the leader of the highest revenue-producing group in the region.

He built an empire of sales managers and his group's revenue continually climbed. Achieving a robust top line, this captain believed he was "in control" of his business. He encouraged his team to do whatever it took to make customers happy and get the sale. They proceeded to do just that.

As revenue climbed, so did Marty's reputation across his region and the entire company.

However, Marty was *selectively* focused on revenue generation and the top line. His leadership began to grow increasingly concerned about his lack of attention to the bottom line.

Marty remained optimistic and sailed forward, convinced his top-line strategy would take care of the bottom line and that he would prevail in the end.

At the end of the year, while the numbers revealed Marty's revenue was indeed sky-high, the financials also showed he was the *least* profitable sales leader in his region.

How could that possibly happen?

Optimism led Marty to believe his strategy of "recruit more salespeople, sell more products, gain more revenue" was the way to achieve the dream. He was selectively obsessed with increasing sales and irrationally blinded to the degradation of margins with each new sales professional he brought on board. His empire of sales professionals also produced significant expenses. Following Marty's encouragement to "do what it takes to make the sale," they wined and dined each customer at the expense of profitability.

Like many Captains of Sails, Marty's optimism was compromised by selective perception. Optimistically and selectively focused on his goal to be the top revenue-producing business in the region, sadly, he became its top *expense-producing* business!

Selective perception is a *partial* interpretation of reality. It's a filtering process that tempts leaders to latch onto favored information, like booming sales, and set aside less appealing information, like booming expenses. Because of unmanaged optimism and selective perception, Marty created his own "reality." His selective focus on his top line created the perception of a top-performing business while, in reality, his bottom line sank his boat's performance.

NAVIGATION KNOTS AND TACKS

"The pessimist complains about the wind. The optimist expects to change it. The leader adjusts the sails."
—JOHN C. MAXWELL

The Captain's Compass shows safe routes for these leaders—one inspired by integrity at the west point, and a countering option supported by the perspective of pessimism at the south point. The east point promises the compounding danger of sailing under the illusion of control. Understanding the directional nature of these biases provides Captains of Sails with the opportunity to adjust their course and outcome.

Optimism Bias

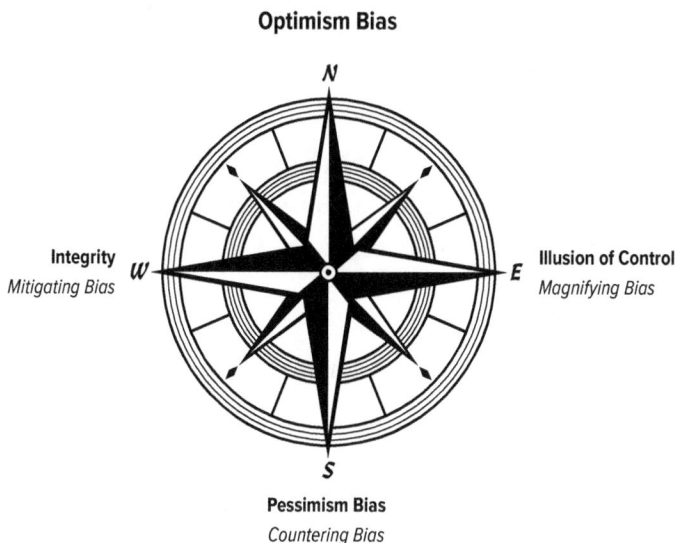

The Captain's Compass: Captains of Sails

The North Cardinal Point: The Optimism Bias

As we have seen, optimism can steer Captains of Sails into perilous situations when unmanaged. Yet, when swayed in the direction of certain biases that offer characteristics that can realistically empower optimism, these captains can prevail.

The East Cardinal Point: Magnifying Mind Knot
Illusion of Control

An illusion of control is a serious threat when conspiring with optimism bias. As we saw with the honorable Captain Billy Tyne and the misguided Captain Marty, judgment and decision-making are negatively affected under the influence of these knots.

An illusion of control fosters an illusion of invincibility. It urges these leaders to forge ahead, believing they are in command and have power over their sail, consequently minimizing threats and risks.

The positive sway of optimism convinces these leaders that they are far more likely to achieve success than experience failure. Under the illusion of control, their minds are bound to believing they have control of factors over which they have absolutely none.

The West Cardinal Point: Mitigating Mind Knot

Integrity

The integrity mind knot can help these captains steer clear of unsavory danger. While integrity is not technically a cognitive bias, for many, it is a deep-seated characteristic that subconsciously guides their judgment, decisions, and behaviors. For others, integrity remains elusive, or as in the case of Captain Crowhurst, is thrown overboard because of tangled thinking and misguidedly optimistic objectives.

We can surmise that Captain Crowhurst's outcome would have been different if his integrity were onboard. Instead, he succumbed to a powerful web of colluding biases that collectively urged him to shift into deception. He weaved a web of untruths and found himself in a bind.

Integrity could have saved his life. Choosing integrity would have meant facing reality. He would have had to withdraw from the race, given the unfit condition of his boat. Had he made that choice, his wife would have had her husband, their children would have had their dad, and Crowhurst would have emerged as a brave captain who embraced a significant challenge and came through it with his character intact. He could have sailed again.

Sailing within the coordinates of integrity is important for these dream-focused captains. With optimism leading every decision, shortcuts are tempting. Succumbing to this temptation threatens, at a minimum, the success of the sale, and most importantly, customer relationships, organizational reputation, and their own character.

Sailing with integrity brings optimism into the realm of reality—enabling sound choices against the sirens of attractive temptations. While immediate returns may be delayed, the integrity route ensures a far greater long-term value and reward for the captain, the organization, its stakeholders, and customers. It offers these captains a steady voyage forward toward their dream. It's the only way to sail.

The South Cardinal Point: Countering Mind Knot

Pessimism Bias

Optimism imagines and expects the best outcome. Pessimism imagines and expects the worst outcome. Considering the contradictory attributes of pessimism, it can be an effective antidote to irrational optimism.

Let me be clear: neither optimism nor pessimism on their own is ideal. We have seen the downfalls of mismanaged optimism. On the other end of the spectrum, pessimistic thinkers hitch themselves to the status quo, making it impossible to advance a vision or a dream.

However, in good measure, thinking like a pessimist can be an effective tack for Captains of Sails—pulling them down from the clouds long enough to engage in critical and clear thinking. Defensive pessimism is a cognitive strategy that can be effective in countering optimism bias. This counter-bias approach is based on adjusting expectations to a more realistic level in which captains can lower their performance expectations to help them prepare for the worst. This enables these captains to consider threats and develop strategies to mitigate risk. Leveraging defensive pessimism also provides the opportunity to consider alternate routes to the targeted outcome.

Most importantly, pessimism, when working in parallel with optimism bias, can result in *rational optimism*.

NAVIGATING OPTIMISM BIAS

Questions: Know Your Knots

- Can I recall a situation where my optimism about an initiative's success led to unforeseen challenges? How did I handle it, and what did I learn?
- Do I exhibit overconfidence in my own abilities or the abilities of my team, assuming that we can overcome obstacles easily?
- Do I proactively develop contingency plans or risk mitigation strategies for potential negative outcomes, or do I assume things will go as I imagine?

Tacking Techniques

- Question why your optimistic dream may be wrong, and list specific reasons that disprove the assumption.

- Identify specific threats that can compromise the journey including a strong emotional attachment to the dream. Seek input, and insights from team members known for their cautious or pessimistic outlook.
- Chart the "ambitious" route. Assess the probability of success supported by clear evidence.
- List what you can control, what you can't, and why. Imagine the dream drowning. Identify who's going down with it and points of failure.
- Leverage preemptive pessimism to urge preparedness. Develop contingency plans and risk mitigation strategies for pessimistic scenarios.
- Hold on to your integrity, regardless of deteriorating circumstances.

THE RATIONAL SOLUTION

"I always like to look on the optimistic side of life, but I am realistic enough to know that life is a complex matter."
—WALT DISNEY

Rational Optimism
"All our dreams can come true, if we have the courage to pursue them."
—WALT DISNEY

Perhaps there is no better example of a business known for making dreams come true than the magical world of Disney.

Walt Disney was a dreamer and a resilient optimist who persevered despite a very tough start. In pursuit of his dream, Walt worked tirelessly on his vision—the future of animation. Doing his best to keep his studio afloat, he got his first big break with the development of Oswald the Lucky Rabbit. This helped fund his studio and set his dream in motion. However, both Lucky Rabbit and his crew were stolen from him.

Walt Disney did not give up on his dream. His optimism would not let him. Though he encountered setbacks, including the pirating of his early treasure and crew, Disney grabbed the helm and charted a new course. With optimism-inspired courage, passion, and perseverance, Disney's dream came true when he replaced his Lucky Rabbit with his magical Mouse.

Mickey Mouse came to life because Walt had an infectious belief in the future of animation. His optimism was relentless, urging the determination and momentum necessary to finally reach his dream. But he didn't rely only on optimism and hope. He managed waves of pessimism. He navigated the harsh reality of difficulties and setbacks.

He was able to use rational optimism to keep moving forward toward his vision.

Dreams to Outcomes

"Courage is going from failure to failure without losing enthusiasm."
—WINSTON CHURCHILL

Optimism on its own cannot ensure the promise of safe passage to a future possibility or probability. And pessimism on its own would prevent the captain from ever leaving the dock.

Rational optimism is the ideal convergence between the helpful attributes of optimistic thinking and the helpful attributes of pessimistic thinking.

Optimists naturally want to steer clear of dream doubters because they never want the wind taken out of their sails. Ironically, however, considering a pessimistic leaning perspective can often shift the sails for optimists, enhancing their ability to foresee future dangers.

Optimism alone is a fast ship that crashes. Pessimism alone is a ship that never leaves the dock. Combined? Rational optimism sails slow and steady and eventually allows leaders to achieve their dreams.

The Dream "Ketcher" Model: The Way Forward

Ketches are well-proven, long-distance sailboats. They are known to endure heavy ocean weather and are recognized for enabling flexibility in their sail plan.

A key attribute of ketches is that they have two masts: a main mast and a shorter mizzenmast. This two-mast boat offers flexibility and power by adjusting the sails to suit the conditions.

Captains of Sails are dream-catchers. Their main mast is optimism, and the mizzenmast represents the combination of pessimism bias and retrospection. The Dream "Ketcher" Model allows these captains to go the distance with power, support, and the agility to adapt to the realities of circumstances.

"The test of a first-rate intelligence is the ability to hold two opposed ideas in mind at the same time, and still retain the ability to function."
—F. SCOTT FITZGERALD, NOVELIST AND ESSAYIST

The vision for this model is to fortify optimism with the strong support of defensive pessimism, raising awareness of risk. Relevant reflection on past experiences also informs the journey.

Retrospection makes it possible to reconcile optimism and pessimism through relevant learnings from real experiences. Captains can prepare for what is to come by referencing what has already happened.

While mind knots cannot be eliminated from our minds, we can learn how to let them work for instead of against us. By leveraging the best attributes and propensities of our prevalent biases, while consciously adopting key attributes of countering biases, we can sail with clearer minds and eyes.

The rational solution is found in harnessing the power of paradoxical thinking—in this case, balancing the upside of optimism with the upside of pessimism.

The Dream "Ketcher" framework transforms unrestrained optimism into rational optimism, enabling critical thinking and sound decision-making...to bring dreams and outcomes to fruition.

Roy E. Disney "Ketches" Dreams

"The thing that distinguishes us from everybody else, and always has and always will, is our past. The goal is to look over our shoulder and see Snow White and Pinocchio and Dumbo standing there, saying, 'Be this good.'"
—ROY EDWARD DISNEY

Roy Edward Disney, son of Roy O. Disney and nephew of Walt Disney, was the last member of the Disney family to be actively involved in the company. He was referred to as the "soul of the company"— its conscience. Roy was known for looking to the past to define the future of Disney. He used retrospection to steer into uncertainty.

During his tenure—he was active until his death in 2009— Roy Disney helped assemble several companies, including the ABC television network. These companies successfully financed one of Walt's most "crazy" dreams: Disneyland. Roy's leadership also drove the dream of animation forward. This led to the production of three of the company's most successful box office hits: *The Little Mermaid, Beauty and the Beast,* and *The Lion King.*

In many respects, Roy was the company's savior, never losing sight of both the positive *and* negative possibilities for the future of Disney. He knew that understanding Disney's past was critical to keep the dream moving forward. He combined optimistic dreams with cautious thinking to create new and successful outcomes.

Roy made dreams come true. He was Disney's guiding beacon in the new "golden age of animation." Never letting his optimism waver, he recognized threats to the company, and with a retrospective mindset, he was the key to the Magic Kingdom for The Walt Disney Company.

Roy, like his uncle Walt, was a Dream "Ketcher."

Achieving the Dream "Ketcher" Model

For these captains, bridging the gap between the dream and reality depends on well-defined performance objectives, deliberate operating tactics, and specific processes for the captain and the organization.

Creating awareness of optimism bias is only the first step on a journey toward a rational solution. This is not a voyage for these captains to sail alone. The value is in a systemic approach to empower rational optimism across the organization, demanding all hands on deck.

THE BOTTOM LINE: ALL HANDS ON DECK

The Dream "Ketcher" Model can be a solid solution for these captains, with multiplying impact at the organizational level. This model facilitates a rational route to making optimistic dreams come true.

The Dream "Ketcher" Model Mission Objectives

- Transforms unrestrained optimism into rational optimism.
- Harnesses the power of optimism to change optimistic possibilities into probable outcomes, leveraging an equal force of optimistic, pessimistic, and reflective thinking— yielding critical thinking, rational judgment, and strategic competitive advantage.

The Strategy Equation

Optimism Bias + Pessimism Bias =
The Dream "Ketcher" Model

Strategic Maneuvers and Organizational Guidance: The Dream "Ketcher" Model

The Dream "Ketcher" Model leverages value drivers of optimism bias including vision, motivation, drive, and resilience alongside value drivers of pessimism bias, risk aversion, and preparedness, along with important characteristics of retrospection. The objective is rational optimism.

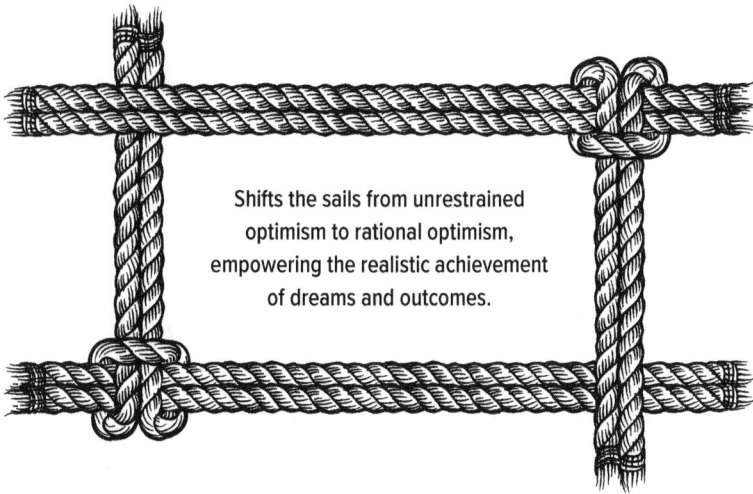

Shifts the sails from unrestrained optimism to rational optimism, empowering the realistic achievement of dreams and outcomes.

The Captain

- *Strategically* optimize optimism. Determine when optimism best serves the company and when it does not.
- Evangelize a "play to win" mindset that empowers optimism with realism.
- Institute a decision framework designed to counter optimism bias, with defensive pessimism, retrospection, and risk management.
- Implement practical organizational interventions that support *rational* optimism through practices anchored in defensive pessimism and preparedness to guard against unbridled optimism.

- Engage a coach to help develop paradoxical thinking as a muscle and strategic personal asset.
- Recruit a risk-management business partner who, appreciating the captain's optimism bias, will work to operationalize the captain's vision, through realism, managed emotion, and integrity.

The Crew—Leadership Team

- Conduct sprints where teams actively seek out potential pitfalls and challenges to optimistic objectives of an initiative.
- Harness realistic perspectives and filter plans through lenses of pessimism and retrospection, enabling risk preparedness and charting contingency routes while respecting the captain's optimistic vision.
- Support teams with training focused on agile thinking strategies and contextual decision frameworks, protecting the value of optimism through the value of defensive pessimism.
- Before decisions are made, reflect on previous initiatives where signals or risks were missed that could have prevented failed missions by invoking caution in judgment.

People Processes

- Assess the optimism bias quotient across the organization to inform a counter-bias intervention strategy with navigational buoys, protecting the organization and culture from potentially damaging effects of optimism bias.
- Balance teams, representing optimistic, pessimistic, and realistic perspectives to optimize for rational decision-making.

- Review hiring processes, integrating an assessment approach identifying optimism bias. Leverage insights for decisions related to selection, coaching, and development to harness an individual's optimism effectively.
- Develop an optimism awareness and training program, highlighting the upside and downside potential of optimism. Integrate training modules including emotional intelligence, defensive pessimism, retrospection, and integrity, highlighting the important role each plays in achieving rational optimism.

Financial Considerations

- Support the captain's optimistic vision and goals with a realistic financial model, illustrating the potential value creation opportunity for the organization. Evaluate plan details and targeted outcomes with quantifiable projections, including financial risk.
- Develop an *optimism*-sensitive forecasting program that brings into focus the viability of ambitious projections through a three-dimensional lens capturing expectation, risk, and retrospection.
- Illustrate financial risk associated with operating plans relative to costs, highlighting the potential impact on margins and profitability.

Commercial Considerations

- Adopt a cross-functional meeting cadence, ensuring integrated business planning and forecasting, realistic customer deliverables, and metrics-driven operating plans exist to support expectations.

- Form a commercial messaging team to audit all marketing communication for reasonableness, accuracy, and prudent promises.
- Ensure a sound decision process for product initiatives, blending optimistic and pessimistic leaning perspectives, improving judgment and understanding of potential positive and negative impact on the business.

Board Considerations

- Adapt board presentations, requiring an upside and downside view of optimistic initiatives, demonstrating strategic reasoning and planning.
- Use independent reviews and assessments to assess the realism of optimistic strategic initiatives and plans.
- Require a risk assessment report throughout operating plan execution.

Five Questions to Identify Indicators of Optimism Bias

1. Thinking back on significant decisions you've made in your leadership role, how often have the outcomes aligned with your initial predictions? Are there instances where your optimistic outlook may have influenced your decisions?

2. When setting a strategic direction or vision for your team or organization, how do you account for potential setbacks or challenges?

3. When considering major decisions or changes, how do you assess and prepare for potential risks? Have there

been times when your initial assessment underestimated certain risks?

4. Describe a time when you allocated resources based on your projections. Did the resources match the actual needs or were adjustments required?

5. How do you communicate expected outcomes and set expectations for your team? Can you recall a time when the team's results vastly differed from your expectations?

TAKEAWAYS: TYING IT ALL TOGETHER

Captains of Sails

Captains of Sails pursue dreams—their own and those of others—with optimism leading the way. They sail to create movement, momentum, and to fulfill dreams, though under the influence of optimism, they may not consider the risks, leaving them unprepared to course correct when necessary.

Optimism Bias

Optimism bias is one of the most prevalent biases. It is not easily managed. Like a gale force wind, optimism can sweep leaders into stormy seas, misdirecting and compromising their vision and mission. It can cause leaders to dismiss risk, ensnaring good judgment and leading to reckless decision-making.

Yet, optimism is key to positive perseverance. This mind knot invokes emotional positivity, causing these captains to stay focused on achieving the dream.

The Rational Solution: The Dream "Ketcher" Model

This model offers a framework that values the power of optimism, and in equal measure, respects the value of defensive pessimism and reflection—the combination of which provides a rational way forward to achieving optimal outcomes for Captains of Sails and their organizations.

SEVEN

THE BELIEF BIAS

S TARTING IN THE EARLY 1800S, UP THROUGH THE 1940s, big paddle-wheeled "showboats" traveled America's waterways, particularly the Mississippi and Ohio Rivers. Carrying troupes of actors and performers, these riverboats were basically floating hotels and theaters. They later began to offer circus, musical, and vaudeville shows, among others. By the 1900s, showboats had evolved into elaborate waterborne palaces attracting sophisticated audiences before they largely faded away by mid-century.

These luxury floating theaters gave rise to the term "showboat," typically referring to someone who intentionally behaves in an extravagant or conspicuous way, regardless of costs. We often hear the term used in sports when athletes engage in boastful behavior, oftentimes ahead of winning. In some cases, we might refer to an athlete or person as having a "showboating style," such as the great Muhammad Ali.

But we see showboating in business as well, behaviors by executives who enjoy attention and the limelight.

THE BELIEF BIAS

*"By believing passionately in something that still
does not exist, we create it. The nonexistent is
whatever we have not sufficiently desired."*

—FRANZ KAFKA, BOHEMIAN NOVELIST

Belief bias binds our perception of arguments, urging us to base our reasoning on the believability of a proposed outcome, rather than on the logical strength of the argument or explanation.

That means that examining the validity of an idea from a logical perspective may not necessarily have any importance at all *when we are inclined to believe.*

When reasoning and logic are submerged, it's easy to latch onto ideas that align with our own beliefs. This belief bind can impel leaders to accept ideas presented by others, even if the details and the "why" behind the ideas are weak. This is particularly true when the idea matches their own belief system, and they believe the outcome makes sense even if the argument doesn't. We are more likely to accept a conclusion as true if it is believable on a personal level, while ignoring logical principles. And this is *because belief is largely tied to emotion.*

Unmanaged, this subjective slant typically results in resistance to changing circumstances or new information that contradicts a preexisting belief. This mind knot also hinders problem-solving by limiting a captain's ability to think outside their own belief bay, which is necessary for creating innovative solutions. And blind belief inevitably causes interpersonal conflicts due to a lack of receptiveness or active listening to the perspectives of others, resulting in missed opportunities and limiting an organization's success and effectiveness.

Through the lens of Captains of Showboating, leaders who perform to persuade, we'll examine the prominent bias to which they are bound – the belief bias.

CAPTAINS OF SHOWBOATING

Captains of Showboating, like the performers aboard the floating theaters of years past, perform grandiosely for others. Sometimes they can be showy swaggerers, captivating the attention of their audience through their not-so-subtle charm. Other times, though their performance may be more subdued, the skillful Captain of Showboating can deliver a spectacular performance and message to their welcoming audience, always aiming to turn them into believers.

Leveraging relationships and trust, and endowed with energy and enthusiasm, Captains of Showboating are audience engagers. With their presence and mastery of messaging, they magnetically command the attention of their onlookers. These leaders believe in their own performances, as well as their ability to cultivate followers.

Some showboating captains believe in the value of transactional performances, delighting their audience with clear solutions to clear problems. Other showboating captains perform for long-term value. They can be visionaries. Immersing themselves in their market, they envision oceans of possibilities—solutions to unanswered needs that can change the game for their audiences' businesses as well as their own.

Let's explore these very different belief-bound Captains of Showboating.

Showboating and Functional Fixedness

Some showboating captains build their believers in the shallows, meaning they transact one performance after another. They're fully engaged in their current show, sometimes with little certainty of the next act or for whom they will be performing.

Mostly outgoing and often impulsive, they are natural entertainers, and they tend to be tactical belief builders. These leaders focus on getting others to believe in the face value of the idea, product, or service they are selling. They rely on their fascinating performance to make believers of their audience, resulting in an immediate return, which is their focus. They often perform for a present payoff versus a future fortune.

These Captains of Showboating are focused on ideas, products, or services that exist in the here and now. What they are "selling" is commonly known, its purpose and application is clear. Their customers are easily converted based on the context and belief in their relationship, as well as their belief in what they are being sold.

Often these captains have a colluding bias known as Functional Fixedness. This mind knot conditions captains and their audience to perceive the functionality of a product or service only in the way in which it is conventionally used. Functional fixedness keeps leaders tied in place, restricting their capability to envision applications of an offering beyond its common use. As a result, these captains tend to serve markets in which they have a clear and consistent product suite, for a clear and conventional audience.

For transaction-oriented Captains of Showboating, a functional fixedness mental tether may help by keeping them focused on the straightforward value they provide to their audience. On the other hand, functional fixedness will negatively affect their ability to problem-solve for audiences who are interested in innovative solutions that market changes require. These captains are fixed on traditional products and services that solve specific problems for customers who use their offerings in conventional ways. Customization is not part of their traditional act. Venturing into uncharted territory introduces risk and can result in failed performances.

These captains have strong interpersonal skills, keeping them center stage in their formal performances or in social situations. Often on the "streetwise" side of the intelligence continuum, these showboaters follow their instinct over information. Immediate gratification and spontaneity drive them to focus on short acts with immediate results, limiting longer-cycle performances with protracted payoffs.

Francesco Schettino—The Captain of Shallow Showboating

On January 13, 2012, Captain Francesco Schettino sailed the luxury cruise liner *Costa Concordia* to disaster, capsizing the 114,500-ton ship when it struck underwater rocks just off Isola del Giglio, Tuscany. Schettino, with Costa Cruises for eleven years, showboated his way into a shipwreck and subsequently jail. Following an extensive investigation of his behavior before, during, and after the incident, Schettino was convicted and sentenced to sixteen years in an Italian prison.

This Captain of Showboating made the poor decision to deviate from the fixed, consistent, and planned route and instead cruised extremely close to the coast of the Tuscan island to show off and "put on a salute" for the people on shore. He believed his short-sighted, shallow water performance, focused on pleasing his admiring audiences on the ship and the coast, would pay immediate dividends without harming the cruise.

This is how it went instead.

Nearing the coast of Tuscany, Schettino summoned his head waiter to the bridge as planned, to give him a spectacular waterside view of his home, while Schettino entertained his non-paying romantic partner, a Moldovan dancer, on the captain's bridge.

The *Costa Concordia* struck the rocks, and, while panicked passengers were scrambling into life jackets, Schettino ordered dinner. Diminishing the severity of the incident, he proceeded to advise the harbormaster that the ship had taken water through an opening in the port side, and he requested a tugboat for assistance. Port authorities were not alerted to the collision until at least an hour after impact, and the order to evacuate the ship was not given until another forty minutes had passed. Schettino disgracefully left the ship in a lifeboat, abandoning at least 300 passengers on board, refusing to return, though urged to do so.

Schettino's performance indeed resulted in a remarkable finale—though not the one he planned. In the final scene, the *Costa Concordia* was destroyed, resulting in thirty-two deaths and a total cost estimated to be approximately $2 billion. Schettino was found guilty of manslaughter and sentenced to sixteen years in prison. This Captain of Showboating let his belief in the short act and his focus on the present overshadow logical reasoning and focus on the long-term mission.

Belief bias latched Schettino's mind to his enticing and plausible performance. His emotional leaning and misjudgment proved to be the authority anchor which gravely tilted his thinking, destroying lives and his ship.

This story demonstrates how the power of belief bias hitched to emotion overshadows rational thinking. It illustrates that an unchallenged belief in an outcome can overtake the long-term value of the mission and the organization.

The next example illustrates the way in which belief bias can cause distortions in the minds of these captains, and perception perplexity, knotting the minds of stakeholders and investors.

WeWrecked

Before his forced resignation in September 2019, Adam Neumann, co-founder of WeWork, a coworking office-space rental company he launched in 2010, showboated his way to a company valuation of $47 billion by January 2019. Newmann proved to be a brazen Captain of Showboating—a firm believer in his grand vision, and a showboating performer who was effective in converting audiences into believers.

This Captain of Showboating came straight from central casting. Standing 6'5", with a charismatic presence, enthusiasm, and masterful performance skills, and even great hair (as many have commented), he might be better characterized as a master illusionist and *make-believer*. His showboating bedazzled his audiences, including celebrities, the media, and his investors.

Neumann's vision and ideals were lofty and expansive, yet his company barely stayed afloat. From his shallow leadership to his shallow promises to WeWork's valuation in the billions,

Neumann showboated his way to a host of problems, and ultimately disaster.

With unwavering belief, and intent on promoting the idealism of WeWork and the multiple other "We" businesses he conceived and believed in, Neumann was truly a masterful performer who was also prone to the Illusion of Validity bias.

An illusion of validity mind knot will provoke a leader to overrate their ability to make accurate predictions. This mental snare impelled Neumann and his investors to subjectively interpret data in such a way that it strengthened their predictions of the company's ostensible colossal success.

Neumann was a Captain of Showboating through and through. His masterful and mind-capturing performances in pitching his WeWork real estate concept as the next big tech bet reeled in two extremely powerful investors: Jamie Dimon, CEO of JP Morgan, who was Neumann's first investor, and Masayoshi Son, CEO of SoftBank. Masayoshi, in less than one hour of witnessing Neumann's wildly optimistic bluster, became a *believer* and promptly invested heavily in the company, which opened the global stage for WeWork.

Belief, Probability, and Distortion

The phenomenon of distortion in probability weighting is one of the many areas behavioral economics experts tackle in examining failures in judgment and decision-making. Noted as one of the more irrational aspects of behavior, it has real-world importance.

Interestingly, as the science of behavioral economics points out, the *smaller* the probability of something occurring, the more we tend to *overestimate* its likelihood. Why? Because we want to believe. Thus, Neumann's overestimation of WeWork's communal officing concept overtaking the global world of office real estate was arguably possible, though not probable. And yet, the company's valuation rose to nearly $50 billion—a classic example of the illusion of validity.

How did that happen?

Despite Neumann's showy propositions of WeWork being a technology company, he actually leveraged a simple business model—renting office space from landlords, breaking the space up into small spaces, and creating flexible workspaces, which he then sublet at a profit. But what Neumann sold to his investors was not a real estate model. Rather, he crafted a captivating WeWork story—a tale of elevating "the world's state of consciousness with a generation of emotionally intelligent entrepreneurs." And his investors believed him.

As a result of Neumann's showboating mastery, WeWork achieved a nearly $50 billion valuation before its free fall to approximately $5 billion. Throughout this captain's journey, losses consistently exceeded revenue. Only a true showboater could sell a net loss of almost $1 billion. And yet, acting with tremendous hubris, Neumann kept the show going, putting on one strong performance after another, gaining ever more believers.

Promising market domination for this communal workspace concept and company, and with the mission to "create a world where people make a life and not just a living," Neumann created a believable illusion that WeWork would take over the global workplace.

Leveraging what he referred to as the *"WeGeneration,"* Neumann imagined a world where people would not be tied to one office location. Rather, they would have a *We* membership enabling free movement around the globe, where a desk would be waiting for them.

But his belief was even broader than that. Changing the company's name to *WeCompany*, his ambitions moved beyond sharing offices to sharing the "human experience" from living space (*WeLive*), to schools (*WeGrow*), to retail (*WeMRKT*). This was an astonishing grand illusion he implanted into the minds of his believers, assuring them they could be participants in a "grand fusion of profit and purpose—a capitalist kibbutz." You certainly couldn't accuse this ultra-realtor of a lack of imagination.

Neumann preached mission, values, and purpose but performed for personal profit. Trademarking the name *WeCompany* early on in his journey, he attempted to take a $6 million fee when the decision was made to adopt the name. Neumann also bought several of the properties on which WeWork operated and leased the space back to his company for millions of dollars. And then there was his acquisition of a $60 million private jet on which he showboated his partying performances while he was flying *high* in the sky. His eccentric behavior included heavy drug use, alcohol, music-dominated office parties, and shooting $140 tequila shots with his "bros" during office meetings.

Blue Ocean Showboating

And then there are the Captains of Showboating who showboat with far more depth. Also believers, and equally gifted and effective in their performances, these captains deliver their belief and vision with an elevated level of sophistication.

Known for their acute perception and optimism, these Captains of Showboating tend to have superior commercial acumen. They can take the simplest form of something and transform it into new and elevated versions. Solution-driven, they are "blue ocean" Captains of Showboating, focused on creative and innovative solutions for enduring future outcomes.

With an extraordinary sense of perception, they can instinctively grasp the important elements of a situation. Their ability to read people and quickly develop valuable insights enables them to support their professional and inspiring performances and propositions with seeming logic.

Steve Jobs was this kind of showboating captain. His belief, supported by his acute market sense and vision, provoked the emergence of products that became solutions and obsessions that the market, his eventual loyal and enduring Apple customers, didn't even know they needed.

In his book, *What the CEO Wants You to Know: How Your Company Really Works*, Ram Charan underscores the invention of the first personal computer, created by Steve Wozniak and Jobs, who "had the ability to see the moneymaking potential of a machine that promised independence and freedom." While all the components for making the computer existed in the market, Jobs had the exceptional vision to pull the pieces together in a way no one else had imagined.

Catching office-automation leaders off guard, the first personal computer was introduced in 1976. As a result of Jobs's prescience, marketing genius, and showboating skills, Apple made money in its first month and hit a billion dollars in sales within ten years. This captain had the blue ocean showboating skills that allowed him to navigate successfully for the long journey and toward sustainable outcomes.

BELIEF COLLUDING BIASES

The Overconfidence Bias

The overconfidence bias is a common colluder with many of the mind knots we talk about in this book. It is a common bias that can lead to uncommon outcomes. Oftentimes it causes unfavorable outcomes, such as the leading role it played in the demise of Captains Schettino and Neumann. Fewer times, overconfidence can play a role in outcomes that are overwhelmingly positive, as in the case of Jobs.

This mind knot can be observed when a captain's confidence in their ability is far greater than what would seem possible for them. Excessive risk-taking is generally associated with leaders who hold this bias, and some would say it is a strong partner to the belief bias held by many entrepreneurs and documented by the high number of such captains who enter a market with low chances of success.

Projection Bias

Projection bias occurs when one gets tangled up in over-predicting that future tastes or preferences will match current tastes or preferences. Adam Neumann's many projections, not the least of which was an incredibly oversized valuation of WeWork as an enduring concept and business model, were based on his belief in a growing taste for communal office space and other communal experiences. Neumann was obsessed with the belief in "We" in everything from communal officing to communal living, communal growing through education and just about anything else to which he could attach "We." He projected the world's taste for communal *everything* would sustain well into the future.

Affect Bias

Affect Bias, another colluder with the belief bias, elevates emotion in the equation, increasing the odds of irrational behavior. This mind knot plays right into the vulnerability of many Captains of Showboating driven by emotion and prone to emotional riptides that lead to shortcut thinking and poor judgment. In other words, emotional response or "affect" takes center stage in decision-making.

This mind knot steers toward a quick path to action, circumventing exhaustive research and deep thinking. Affect bias subconsciously reduces cognitive load by avoiding logical decision-making.

It works like this. When these captains have positive feelings toward an action, any potential risk will be considered low, while benefits will be believed to be high. On the other hand, when feelings toward an activity are negative, these captains will believe risk to be high and consider any potential benefit to be low.

NAVIGATION KNOTS AND TACKS

There are two key maneuvers these captains can make to tame their belief bias which can keep Captains of Showboating credibly converting believers—leveraging social proof and countering their belief by considering the regret they may feel if their belief is wrong. Optimism, at the east cardinal point, will conspire to heighten their risk.

Belief Bias

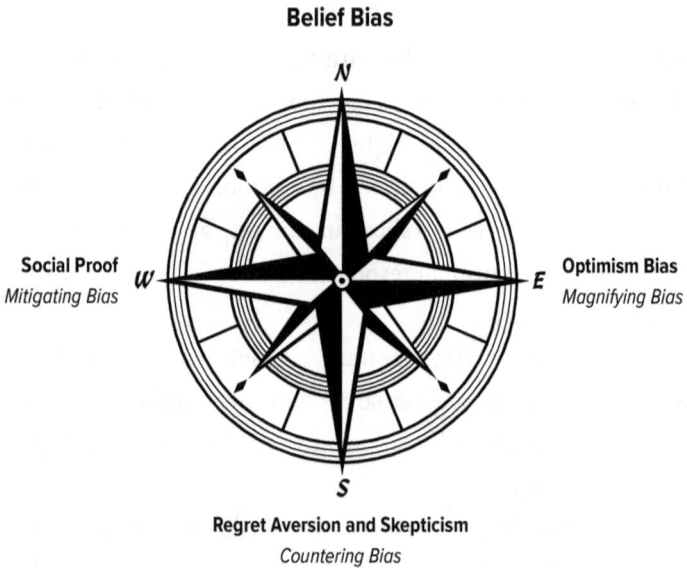

Social Proof
Mitigating Bias

W

E

Optimism Bias
Magnifying Bias

Regret Aversion and Skepticism
Countering Bias

The Captain's Compass – Captains of Showboating

The North Cardinal Point: Belief Bias

Belief bias, positioned at the north cardinal point, is often a prominent mind knot for Captains of Showboating. When this mind knot is in play, reasoning is not based on the strength of an argument, but on the plausibility and believability of the conclusion. This knot binds us to our own belief system, making us more likely to accept the outcome of something if it matches what we believe. And even if an argument is confusing, bearing no real logic, we often believe that, if the conclusion seems to make sense based on our beliefs, this mind knot will move our mind past the flawed and frayed argument to the *believable* conclusion we like.

The East Cardinal Point: Magnifying Mind Knot

The Optimism Bias

Optimism bias typically creates a decisional double knot for Captains of Showboating, making their ingrained beliefs even stronger—causing them to move forward with even greater conviction. Moving full steam ahead, with rose-tinted glasses, these optimistically inspired Captains of Showboating believe the impossible can be done. To gain believers, showboating captains often overstate possibilities out of sheer optimism.

Optimism nurtures and shapes the development of customer networks for these captains, confidently believing in their ability to deliver both a winning performance and solution.

Cognitive neuroscientist Tali Sharot, author of *The Optimism Bias: A Tour of the Irrationally Positive Brain*, acknowledges the prevalence of the emotional oar of optimism. She highlights the many benefits of optimism, including its confidence-boosting effect. As we've seen in this chapter, and as Sharot also notes, optimism plays a significant role in urging risky behavior that can result in negative outcomes.

Optimism magnifies the effect of belief bias for these Captains of Showboating, tethering them to the optimistic outcome they seek.

The West Cardinal Point: Mitigating Mind Knot
Social Proof

Captains of Showboating thrive based on their ability to influence and sway social approval of their customers and markets. They are not only energized by their audience but also depend on others' belief. Public recognition and endorsement are key to their success. Without their ability to influence and convert their audiences into believers, Captains of Showboating become ineffective. In his book, *Influence*, Robert Cialdini created the term "Social Proof" to capture the phenomenon in which people copy the actions and behaviors of others in a given situation.

The social proof bias, well-recognized in behavioral economics and finance, can be a powerful tool to promote evidence-based thinking and mitigate belief bias.

Captains who slow down to consider the social sentiment of their audience give themselves the space to assess the effect of their emotionally spirited, *belief-based performance*. They can determine whether they are propelling their mission or not, based on their audience's social feedback. When they sense rejection, or a lack of social proof signals, they may be inspired to reframe their performance, showcasing *evidence-based beliefs* in support of their desired outcome. The benefit for these captains is that slower processing time is more likely to yield logical rather than belief-based outcomes.

High social acceptance, whether from investors or customers, compounds the belief and commitment these leaders have to their vision. Likewise, low social acceptance translates to rejection and can powerfully urge these captains to leverage logic and evidence-based beliefs to strengthen their social sway. Captains of Showboating need believers to succeed. If they are not converting their audience into believers, they will find themselves in their farewell act.

The South Cardinal Point: Countering Mind Knot

Regret Aversion

Regret Aversion is fear-based, while belief bias largely ignores or dismisses fear. Regret aversion can play a role in transforming a strong belief bias.

First, let's explore the psychological bias of regret aversion. This cognitive coil often pushes away opportunities that offer a positive outcome, fearing that the possibility of a negative outcome would lead to regret in the future. Directed by this bias, captains will avoid taking a certain action, fearing the risk that their action will result in a negative outcome—*even if the potential positive outcome outweighs the risk.*

Unlike many mental shortcuts that prioritize "in the moment" thinking, regret aversion influences decisions through a future lens based on the fear of experiencing potential regret after a decision is made. Consequently, captains may make decisions in the present, abandoning good thinking to avoid the potential future regret of making an alternate decision. An example would be decision-making based on the "Fear of Missing Out," or FOMO.

Leveraging this fear-based bias and its *future-feeling influence,* regret aversion can be an effective counteracting mind knot to belief bias. Belief is rarely based on logic, critical thinking, or good reasoning. Instead, it hijacks our minds based on a compelling positive *feeling* associated with something to which we are blindly committed. Regret aversion can also cause us to abandon good reasoning, except we do so hijacked by the fear of a potentially compelling negative *feeling* and the discomfort we fear we'll feel if we commit to the wrong thing.

Tapping into their fear of *bad feelings* associated with potential future regret can urge these captains to question the merits of the *good feelings* associated with their beliefs. Remember, science shows fear of loss is a stronger driver than potential gain. Therefore, regret aversion can be an effective belief challenger for these captains, pushing them to scrutinize their belief for fear of the inevitable regret they will feel if they steer in the wrong direction.

Skepticism

Skepticism, while not a formally recognized bias in behavioral economics, is nonetheless an impactful mind knot that affects leaders in different ways.

When leveraged constructively, skepticism questions the validity or authenticity of something that is purported to be factual or sound. Captains who are skeptics ensure they have evidence before making claims and scrutinize information for logical soundness. They understand the burden of proof rests with the person making the claim. Attributes of skepticism can counteract belief bias by urging evidence-based thinking.

Too often skepticism is considered to be a form of pessimism. Yet, skepticism is distinctly different from pessimism.

Pessimism bias causes us to overestimate the likelihood that negative things *will happen*, and positive things *will not*. Skepticism is not bound to negative thinking, nor does it indicate outright disbelief. Rather, it drives critical thinking. Skepticism slants thinking toward a process of *supporting* an unknown conclusion, rather than *justifying* a preconceived one. A skeptic explores to understand, rather than to defend, an existing belief. It provides a filtering process for over-projections and overestimations, to which Captains of Showboating are prone.

Captains of Showboating thrive on delivering performances to promote their vision and to convert their audience into believers. Skeptical audiences can dampen the energy and enthusiasm of these leaders, negatively affecting their performance and ability to attract and convert believers.

Skepticism is an effective filter for beliefs that are overly ambitious and often overestimated. It can go a long way toward bringing these Captains of Showboating down from idealistic "blue sky" thinking and grounding them in some level of pragmatism and reality. Skepticism can urge them to navigate more strategically, avoiding potential storms, and even identifying more beneficial routes toward the outcome they seek.

NAVIGATING BELIEF BIAS

Questions: Know Your Knots

- Am I more likely to accept arguments and ideas that align with my existing beliefs, even if they lack strong evidence?
- Do I distinguish between facts and opinions when evaluating arguments and evidence, and do I prioritize facts over beliefs?
- Do I recognize when my emotional attachment to certain beliefs may be clouding my judgment and influencing my assessment of arguments?

- When presented with compelling evidence that challenges my beliefs, am I willing to adjust my views accordingly?
- Do I practice intellectual humility? Am I open to acknowledging that I may not have all the answers and that my beliefs are subject to change as I learn more?

Tacking Techniques

- Actively seek information and engage others in debates and discussions, exposing yourself to different viewpoints to refine your skeptical skills.
- Link emotionally inspired performances to evidence-based scripts.
- Adjust the "performance" to create enthusiasm for evidence as well as excitement for the proposed outcome.
- Diversify sources of information and actively seek out a variety of perspectives when researching or evaluating arguments.
- Weigh the potential consequences of not addressing risk by analyzing potential negative outcomes.
- Develop clear criteria to challenge beliefs and "probable" outcomes.
- Consider potential future regret if the mission doesn't go as believed.
- Form a skeptics committee of "belief challengers" tasked with challenging prevailing beliefs, uncovering weaknesses in arguments, and presenting alternate viewpoints.

THE RATIONAL SOLUTION

Transcending the Irrationality of Belief Bias

Belief steers thinking and the intensity of commitment to an idea or endeavor, not because of a sound argument, but by triggering acceptance of an argument because the proposed outcome aligns to one's belief system. Consequently, this belief mind knot leads to wrong conclusions and even disastrous outcomes due to flawed reasoning.

However, the power of belief cannot be overlooked when it comes to the achievement of excellent and even extraordinary outcomes. So, how do Captains of Showboating benefit from their belief bias while transcending its irrational sway?

Just what is it that differentiates the showboating captains who fail to achieve the outcomes they promise in their stellar performances from those who deliver the outcomes they promise, and sometimes, outcomes that even exceed their believers' expectations?

Let's look at a Captain of Showboating who successfully transitioned his belief into reality, one cup at a time.

Howard Schultz and the Voyage of the Mystical Mermaid

"This may sound a bit naïve, but I got here
by believing in big dreams."
—HOWARD SCHULTZ

It was the collusion of several mind knots that guided and drove Captain Howard Schultz to pursue his "north star," resulting in his own stardom and that of Starbucks. This is an example of how the integration of the right attributes associated with certain biases and the right captain can have a significant impact on consumers, companies, and markets worldwide. And in this case, it all started with belief bias.

Belief in an extraordinary outcome is what drove the growth and transformation of Starbucks from its modest beginning in Seattle to its stupendous growth and legendary success across the globe. Howard Schultz was a different sort of Captain of Showboating. With heartfelt passion and conviction, Schultz believed in his core, not in what Starbucks *was*, but in what it *could be*. As a result of his unwavering belief in the allure and outcome he foreshadowed, the legendary Starbucks was percolated and consumed in the same way the company was built, "one cup at a time."

As of the third quarter of 2022, the company reported 34,317 retail locations worldwide and revenues of nearly $30 billion.

The original three founders of Starbucks opened their first location in Seattle's Pike Place Market in 1971, selling roasted coffee beans, not cups of coffee. In 1982, they hired 29-year-old Howard Schultz as the director of retail operations and marketing.

Schultz was unable to turn the company's three founders into believers in his vision of transforming the company into a sophisticated Italian café that served authentic espresso. Though Schultz had not yet perfected a compelling performance showboating why Starbucks would rise to supremacy, his intense belief in the product and concept, his transformative vision, and the grand possibilities for the company grew stronger and stronger.

With Starbucks founders' acquisition of Peet's Coffee, the company expanded its footprint of coffee bean shops, though fresh-brewed cups of coffee were still not for sale. Schultz left the company after this acquisition to launch Il Giornale, his own version of an authentic Italian café that served coffee and espresso.

In 1987, the original owners of Starbucks decided to sell their Seattle stores, the roasting plant, and the name Starbucks. Much bigger than Il Giornale, Schultz was compelled to purchase this Starbucks package. Since he had exhausted almost all of his resources in raising the funds he needed to launch Il Giornale, Schultz needed to raise close to another $4 million to acquire Starbucks. He believed he could do it, and he believed he could convince investors to *believe in his vision*. He also believed, if he didn't give it his best shot, he would regret his decision. And that drove him even more.

Though Schultz had performed more than a hundred times during his capital raise for Il Giornale, he practiced and improved his performance for critical meetings with potential investors. "I didn't want to step onstage until I was absolutely prepared."

To his devastating disappointment, he learned one of his investors planned to buy Starbucks out from under him. He approached his remaining investors and gave them the performance of his life. Fueled with unbridled belief, confidence, optimism, and passion, Schultz enchanted them with his vision, and they invested the $3.8 million he needed to successfully purchase Starbucks. He believed, and his dream began to come to life.

Next, he needed to address the management team's poor morale, to convert them into believers in his vision for the company. He also faced the significant decision of whether to choose Il Giornale or Starbucks as the name for the combined business.

Skeptical about making the right choice, Schultz sought the advice and perspective of others. As a result of his thoughtful process, he decided to sail forward with Starbucks and the famous mermaid logo for their combined "mystical sense," which brilliantly suited his vision for the company.

It was the powerful combined biases of belief, overconfidence, and optimism that kept Schultz firmly tied to his vision and his dream. Yet, it was his fear of regret and the humility of skepticism that enabled him to make critical decisions, including his decision to adopt the Starbucks name, which is now an iconic worldwide brand.

Unlike Captain Neumann, Schultz enchanted his investors, employees, and importantly, his customers, absent any illusion. He built an enduring company by fulfilling the alluring promises he made. He showboated and navigated his ship from possibility to probability, and then masterfully to reality.

The Enduring Enchanter Model: The Way Forward

"The goal of enchantment is a long-lasting change—not a one-time sale or transaction... you want enchantment to endure and, even better, to blossom. That's what happens when you change hearts, minds, and actions."
—GUY KAWASAKI, *ENCHANTMENT*

The Enduring Enchanter Model transforms pure believers into thoughtfully cautious decision-makers and action-takers. It is based on the decision-processing combination of belief, regret avoidance, and the humility of skepticism, setting these believing captains apart.

The model provides a framework that enables these captains to achieve the positive outcomes in which they believe. It offers a rational way forward for Captains of Showboating, their believers, and their organizations. It transforms the influential performances of these captains from merely entertaining and engaging to meaningful promises with the probability of successful and enduring outcomes. Core to the model's success is a willingness to challenge beliefs. The model enables these captains to enchant audiences, making them true believers—who in turn become the foundation and reality of the captain's enduring belief.

"Enchanter" describes the ambition and *modus operandi* of Captains of Showboating. These persuading performers sway their spectators toward their belief and vision. Enchanting audiences, whether stakeholders, customers, or investors, showboating captains must present their beliefs and goals, along with evidence others can embrace to become enduring believers.

The Enduring Enchanter Model offers these captains a powerful route to captivate the minds and hearts of their audiences with arguments and promises of integrity, while increasing the probability of the outcomes they espouse.

The key distinction of the Enduring Enchanter Model is the opposition of its value-driving elements—belief bias working in sync with *unbelieving-leaning* drivers of regret aversion and skepticism. Regret aversion can cause these captains to pause and question their belief. Then, skepticism can provide a filtering function by challenging "enchanting" beliefs without dismissing them.

Howard Schultz is a clear example of an Enduring Enchanter.

Captains and Collaboration

Achieving the Enduring Enchanter Model vision is a rational solution for Captains of Showboating. However, these captains cannot do it alone.

While every cognitive bias highlighted in this book is described and examined through the lens of each of the archetypal captains, biases are not a problem for the leader alone. Rather, they can contaminate an organization and certainly its mission.

The vision for the Enduring Enchanter Model is a navigation plan and framework for achieving performance objectives through practical and tactical activities that harness the powerful aspects of belief along with the caution of regret and skepticism for sound navigation to achieving positive outcomes.

For these captains to realize the overall vision, they must engage and collaborate with stakeholders and the organization. Therefore, priorities, performance objectives, and good practices are critical.

THE BOTTOM LINE: ALL HANDS ON DECK

Belief bias, while mostly considered a danger to logical reasoning and decision-making, has certain value-driving attributes that can be instrumental to the success of Captains of Showboating and their organizations. A proactive approach for combating widespread belief bias across an enterprise requires a focus on processes and practices that promote and guide critical thinking and effective decision-making.

Enduring Enchanter Model Objectives

- Harness the power of belief and its positive attributes of commitment, confidence, conviction, and consistency, which inspire trust and confidence among teams across the organization.
- Transform blind belief by leveraging regret aversion and the power of skepticism to strengthen the merit and integrity of ideas and beliefs.

Strategy Equation

Belief Bias + Regret Aversion and Skepticism =
The Enduring Enchanter Model

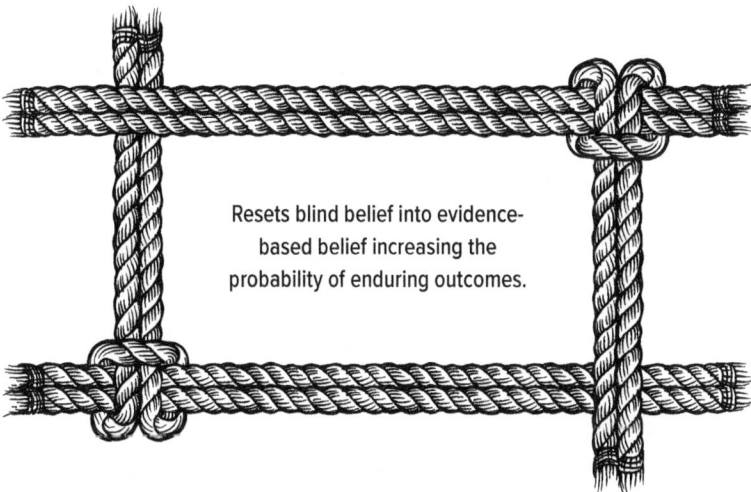

Resets blind belief into evidence-based belief increasing the probability of enduring outcomes.

Strategic Maneuvers and Organizational Guidance:
The Enduring Enchanter Model

The framework is intended as guidance and can serve as inspiration for tailored practices that suit your organization. The model leverages the positive traits of belief bias such as confidence and conviction, and the value of regret aversion, along with the characteristics of skepticism and critical questioning of beliefs, providing a framework for positioning captains and their organizations for better judgment, decision-making, and enduring performances.

The Captain

- Slow down decisions to move forward by considering the potential regret associated with belief-driven decisions. Practice regret-thinking, and invite skepticism into complex and uncertain situations to infuse caution into the decision process.
- Conduct regular self-audits of your own decisionmaking processes to identify instances where belief bias may have influenced your choices.
- Encourage a culture of skepticism and intellectual humility.
- Develop decision frameworks that explicitly incorporate regret aversion, emphasizing the potential negative consequences of belief-driven decisions.
- Integrate perspectives from various backgrounds and experiences to garner diverse thoughts for consideration alongside preexisting beliefs.
- Conduct a regular assessment of decision processes to identify the influence of belief bias. Ensure skepticism and the right measure of regret thinking are engaged to strengthen the integrity of decisions.
- Establish expert panels or committees that provide independent assessments of important decisions,

offering valuable social proof of the importance of evidence-based thinking.

The Crew—Leadership Team

- Develop specific practices to improve critical thinking in information processing to avoid the pitfalls of belief bias.
- Set clear decision-process guidelines that acknowledge personal beliefs and openly examine evidence that disproves the belief.
- Consider utilizing Kanban boards to visualize and manage identified risks and uncertainties associated with prevailing beliefs
- Employ a "regret aversion" mindset to elevate caution. Identify skeptics on the team and encourage an effective filtering process to either validate the belief or counter it.
- Require each team member to raise a challenge to the prevailing belief as a means of stirring critical discussion ahead of a decision.
- Share case studies and examples that illustrate the value of an evidence-based decision process to counter the pitfalls of belief-driven decisions.

People Processes

- Develop organizational training workshops to elevate awareness of belief bias, highlighting its propensities and ability to hijack good decision-making. Ensure training includes modules on evidence-based critical thinking and the value of skepticism in evaluating arguments.

- Adopt an assessment approach to identify indicators of belief bias for use in selection. Leverage tools that can signal belief bias, including flexibility in thinking, resistance to change, appreciating others' perspectives, emotional intelligence, practical thinking, and balanced decision-making.
- Foster a culture of intellectual humility, where individuals are encouraged to acknowledge the limits of their knowledge and be open to changing their minds based on evidence.

Financial Considerations

- Implement regular financial audits conducted by independent experts to ensure that financial decisions are based on sound evidence and skepticism free of a potential cultural belief bias.
- Use data-driven financial modeling to assess various scenarios, challenging prevailing beliefs across the organization.

Commercial Considerations

- Prioritize market research and data-driven analyses in commercial decision-making, highlighting examples of successful outcomes resulting from evidence-based strategies.
- Conduct regular market assessments to evaluate the validity of existing beliefs about customer preferences and market dynamics.
- Evaluate go-to-market assertions and promises to ensure they are not just enchanting but show evidence of enduring solutions.

- Build a sales organization with an appropriate balance of believers and realists to ensure customers are developed confidently, consistently, and credibly through enchanting, evidence-based belief performances for enduring relationships.

Board Considerations

- Require a checks and balances approach to all "enchanting" ideas and initiatives raised by belief-biased Captains of Showboating.
- Require evidence illustrating the merit of the belief, as well as its potential liabilities. Include evidence that the captain has engaged other stakeholders, filtering the belief through a lens of skepticism—considering both the possible regret the organization may face by moving forward as well as any potential lost opportunity by not moving forward.

Five Questions to Identify Indicators of Belief Bias

1. How do you ensure that your decisions aren't overly influenced by preexisting beliefs? Do you consider diverse perspectives and opinions before you make your decision?
2. When presented with a new business strategy or idea, how do you evaluate its validity?
3. How do you handle information or data that contradicts your current understanding or strategy?
4. Can you recall a time when you changed a strongly held belief or strategy based on new evidence or perspectives?

5. How do you handle disagreements within your team, especially when team members present evidence that challenges your prevailing viewpoint?

TAKEAWAYS: TYING IT ALL TOGETHER

Captains of Showboating

Captains of Showboating are unwavering believers. Multifaceted performers skilled in the art of "sway," these captains are usually entertainers, influencers, and vision-sellers capable of swaying minds and hearts, converting their audience into believers, and leveraging the power of emotion and relationships.

Some Captains of Showboating engage in reimagining the ordinary. Focused on the expansion of ideas, products, services, and value-adding solutions, their showboating performances can be magnetic and inspiring, producing positive outcomes.

Captains of Showboating are prominent holders of belief bias, and they are skilled in the art of "sway."

Belief Bias

Belief bias binds leaders to their personal beliefs, absent clear evidence to support their viewpoint, blinding its hosts to information, risk, and other perspectives that may rightly invalidate their belief. It judges an argument's strength not by how strongly it supports the conclusion, but by how plausible the conclusion is in one's own mind.

When managed, belief bias can fuel remarkable outcomes; when unmanaged, it can lead to significant misjudgments and disastrous outcomes. The determining factor is the captain's awareness, mental agility, and ability to adopt strategies to ensure their belief mind knot works in their favor and not against them. This mind knot increases our acceptance of showboating performances more than we would be comfortable admitting.

The Rational Solution: The Enduring Enchanter Model

This model provides a rational route for the Captains of Showboating, who are typically prone to belief bias. The framework honors the determination and fortitude of belief, while managing it with strategies that leverage attributes of regret aversion and behaviors associated with the scrutiny of skepticism. With the proper mental agility to simultaneously leverage the tension and opposition of these mind knots, the Enduring Enchanter Model has the potential to restage blind belief into evidence-based belief, increasing the probability of enduring outcomes. It can guide these captains from being vulnerable believers to becoming astute achievers.

EIGHT

THE INTUITION BIAS

THE GIFT AND GNARL OF INTUITION

*"The intuitive mind is a sacred gift, and the rational
mind is a faithful servant. We have created a society
that honors the servant and has forgotten the gift."*

—ALBERT EINSTEIN

N THIS CHAPTER, WE EXPLORE THE GOOD AND THE BAD
of intuition, the gift and the gnarl, through the lens of intuitive leaders—the Captains of Wayfinding.

The *gift* to which Einstein so aptly referred is the elusive, unconscious power of intuition. Intuition is the ability to know something without *analytic* reasoning. It comes from the Latin word *intueri*, which means to look inside or to contemplate. It is an elusive way of *knowing*. It's been referred to as "a powerful voice that speaks without words."

Intuition arises from a process of pattern-searching and recognition. The intuitive mind will look for a match of an idea or concept in our memory, while our automatic or "shortcut" thinking retrieves a solution that seems to fit the situation in question. And when time allows, our more complex thinking power kicks in to analyze and modify it.

Unlike the logical mind, which leverages a structure or method for reasoning, the intuitive mind has its own processing and decision-making approach. While both approaches include problem definition, analysis, and synthesis, these stages occur far faster in the intuitive mind.

Where a logical process relies on concrete rules and formulas and works in a linear manner, the intuitive process relies on rules and formulas found in experiences and memories. It is far from linear. The intuitive mind moves quickly from side to side, and it all happens on an unconscious level through a complex process of pattern matching and unique associations. Most significantly, the intuitive process is uniquely individualized.

Intuitive judgment is accompanied by a *feeling* that one's instinct is correct, even in the absence of rational analysis.

It's All About Pattern Recognition

While intuition is often referred to as a "gut feeling," we know there is mounting evidence that it's more than just a feeling.

Malcolm Gladwell, author of multiple *New York Times* bestsellers, acknowledges intuition is automatic and unconscious because it is deeply learned expertise. Similarly, Gary Klein, well-respected cognitive psychologist and author of *The Power of Intuition*, writes, "Skilled decision-makers rely on deeply held patterns of learned experience in making quick and efficient decisions." Klein also concludes that intuition is "based on large numbers of patterns gained through experience, resulting in different forms of tacit knowledge."

Tacit knowledge can mean reading between the lines or reading body language, or it can describe things that we do expertly and intuitively, not explainable to others.

Gerd Gigerenzer, a psychologist at the Max Planck Institute for Human Development in Berlin, maintains that even for more complex problems, intuition drives decisions. As an example, he shared his experience working with top executives at the largest German firms. "They go through all the data they have—and they're buried under data—and at the end, the data don't tell them what they should do....[Intuition] is a form of unconscious intelligence that is as needed as conscious intelligence." Based on his work, he believes that in certain circumstances, heuristics, the building blocks of intuition, can lead to better choices.

There have been multiple studies conducted to gain a clearer understanding of how unconscious intuition can inform and even improve decision-making. While many believe business decisions should be based strictly on empirical evidence, the field of neuroscience is increasingly giving credibility and importance to the critical role that intuition plays in decision making and leadership.

An explanation offered by Nobel laureate Herbert Simon describes skilled intuition in this way: "The situation has provided a cue: This cue has given expert access to information stored in memory, and the information provides the answer. Intuition is nothing more and nothing less than recognition."

Modesto A. Maidique, a professor at the Harvard Business School and President Emeritus and Executive Director of the Center for Leadership at Florida International University in Miami, conducted a study where he interviewed CEOs about the role intuition played in their decision-making as well as the outcome of those decisions. His study revealed that intuition was a major or determining factor in 85 percent of thirty-six major CEO decisions explored. Overwhelmingly, the CEOs stated their success rate was several times higher for decisions made in the fields where they had expert knowledge.

Maidique concluded, "If intuition is indeed the handmaiden of experience, it stands to reason that those decision-makers who have passed Herb Simon's 10,000-hour experience threshold would have higher quality intuition. Thus, intuition is more than a feeling, and experience can be a key differentiator."

However, Maidique importantly adds, intuition requires *more* than just domain knowledge. It also requires deep introspection to understand the biases and emotions or "offsets" to the decision-making compass, which may ultimately override domain knowledge and result in poor judgments. He asserts the effectiveness of intuitive decisions is best conveyed in two wise sayings, "Know your business" and "Know yourself." And, I would add, know your knots.

The Practical Value of "Spidey Sense"

Your intuition is different from your conscience... your conscience shouts, "Here's what you should do," while your intuition whispers, "Here's what you could do."

—STEVEN SPIELBERG

"Spidey sense" is the actual term used by the US Office of Naval Research (ONR) to describe intuition or that "added edge" that is so important in high-pressure combat situations when leaders need to act quickly. Intuition helps leaders make better decisions when uncertainty and urgency are the presiding current. ONR went so far as to develop methods to measure the *workings of intuition* on the battlefield to be able to develop intuitive decision-making for military personnel.

Lieutenant Commander Brent Olde of ONR's Warfighter Performance Department for Human and Bioengineered Systems explained, "If we can characterize this intuitive decision-making process and model it, then the hope is to accelerate the acquisition of these skills."

Active military situations are defined by ambiguity, and under such conditions leaders must act quickly. Time spent waiting for data puts the mission at risk. There is a time and a place for analytical decision-making, and it's not on the military battlefield, nor is it in business situations where present uncertainty demands quick decisions. In pre-hostility contingency planning, or in the context of strategic business planning, there is time and room for analysis. Though as the commander points out, "Once you cross the line of departure, data and planning rapidly diminish in usefulness."

Or, as heavyweight champ Mike Tyson so succinctly put it, "Everyone has a plan until they get punched in the mouth." That's when your plan goes out the window, and intuition takes over.

The military understands the power of intuitive muscle. The late Colin Powell, former US secretary of state and a four-star military leader, spoke openly on the topic of "informed intuition."

Powell believed one measure of being an intuitive leader is having both the confidence and ability to rely on a "gut check." He explained that when presented with evidence from those under his command, he challenged himself with key questions: "I know what I'm *supposed* to feel about this. Now what do I *really* feel about this? Do I believe this reality?" Powell was known for his commitment to an important gut-check principle—to look at what the data is telling you and question if it's the same thing that your gut is telling you. If the data and gut are not aligned, then why?

The Downside: The Gnarl of Intuition Bias

Nobel laureate Daniel Kahneman, world-renowned for his work in behavioral economics and finance, and specifically cognitive biases, cautioned that Intuition Bias is the flip side of "good" intuition, and it's often difficult to distinguish.

Kahneman's work helps us to understand the "gnarl" of intuition. "We think we know," he said, "but are we knowing because we recognize a special pattern, or is it more of, 'Hey, that person looks like me or talks like me, so their idea must be good'? Sometimes sources look good because they look familiar. You need to decide if it is bias dressed as intuitive insight."

There are multiple reasons why this mind knot complicates judgment and decision-making.

First, it is simply easier to go with intuition, avoiding the analytical work involved in non-intuitive alternatives. In other cases, an executive may simply lack the interest, capacity, or mental agility required to pursue a highly complex analytical process. And sometimes, it may just be that the executive may refuse to consider that their intuitive feeling may benefit from evidence or intervention.

Another reason intuition may take precedence is due to the Anchoring Bias, which can urge us to anchor on our first impression—or in this case, an immediate intuitive feeling. Staying anchored to an overriding gut sense is the easier route, and it *feels* right. Intuition convinces us that if we ignore our gut, and instead engage in complex data analysis and structured thinking, the resulting outcome could be negative. So why would we do anything different from anchoring to our intuitive option?

Intuition Bias has another precarious strand: it invokes emotion into the equation. We begin to imagine and anticipate how we will feel about consequences, or the outcome of our intuitive choice compared to how we anticipate we would feel about an analytically driven choice. Research studies show that we experience intensified emotions in connection with potential outcomes of gut-driven choices over non-intuitive choices. These feelings exacerbate and reinforce our tendency to lean in the direction of an intuitive decision over an option arrived at through structured analysis.

And when we act on intuition, we experience an elevated sense of responsibility and personal accountability that is both exciting and empowering. We then become personally engaged, compelling us to drive the outcome associated with our intuitive choice.

As much as we value the "gift" of intuition, it can equally be the "gnarl" that prevents rational thinking, causing bad decisions and even catastrophic outcomes.

CAPTAINS OF WAYFINDING

"The first step is intuition and it comes with a burst."
—THOMAS EDISON

Captains of Wayfinding possess the precious gift of intuition—but they're equally vulnerable to the gnarl of this mind knot. These captains are intuitive explorers who are most valued for their ability to navigate well within complexity and environments of change. They have a strong ability to recalibrate and to adjust navigation when necessary.

On the surface, these captains appear to be quick and spontaneous thinkers. In truth, they are integrative processors with a special ability to make decisions and to resolve problems based on gut feeling or their unexplained "knowing," versus following the far narrower channel of rational logic.

Keenly perceptive, these captains have an innate ability to hear what others are not saying, and to see what others are not seeing. They perceive subtle signs and make interconnections enabling them to size up a situation in a way most others would not. Captains of Wayfinding receive special "vibrations" of knowing something without any evidence or proof.

Thomas Edison, who was exceptionally observant and characterized as having an insatiable curiosity, described his influx of insights as arriving with a burst. We know these bursts of genius were driven by ideas, previous experiences, and largely subconscious learning and knowledge, or "vibrations." Edison used the term "intuition" to describe the undercurrent of vibrations that led to his insights. He believed in what he saw, *felt*, and imagined, all of which intuition was reported to inspire.

Captains of Wayfinding are most visible in seas of change when uncertainty is the only thing that is certain.

These are leaders who "get it." And, when they get it, they are resolute in their decisions and actions. These captains excel in times of crisis, transformation, and change when uncertainty and ambiguity prevail, because they can make decisions quickly with imperfect information.

Recognized for their fast thinking and quick decision-making, and often trending against the current, these leaders naturally default to their "invisible" intuition, sometimes leaning more in the direction of risk, where they see reward.

In more stable environments, Captains of Wayfinding are perceived as high-risk takers who lean on intuition at the expense of data. They are widely misunderstood and often frightening to the mass population because they see beyond the status quo to an attractive horizon not visible to others. Most people gravitate to safe places and will resist change if given the opportunity. Wayfinding captains are far less highly regarded in calm waters, where a steady journey to a well-understood destination is both the preference and the mandate.

The 2020 Covid-19 pandemic presented a dramatic and unforeseen reality for captains and their businesses. Companies across the globe faced the challenge of quickly adapting within the context of uncertainty. They either floated, capsized, or flourished depending on their ability to quickly adjust their sails, and in many cases to navigate along a new journey.

Leaders suddenly experienced a screeching halt to their conventional operations. With tremendous uncertainty on the horizon, business savvy was critical to transform, operationalize, and adapt in completely new ways to generate revenue. Having to adapt quickly, logic was not steering the ship. These transformations required new thinking and intuitiveness to steer companies to better outcomes than they faced at the start of the crisis.

For all captains, business savvy was indeed tested. For some it meant steering into uncharted waters, whether repurposing manufacturing operations to produce critical healthcare supplies and protective equipment or overhauling entire supply-chain systems of food manufacturers, grocery, and online retailers. Some figured out a way to leverage their expertise, operations, materials, and time, to respond to the immediate needs of their markets with new products, and in most cases, new delivery systems. The captains of these businesses demonstrated speed of thought, mental and operational agility, innovativeness, and integrative and adaptive thinking.

Savviness, intuition, and mental agility was the call to action, and as we emerged from the height of the crisis, Captains of Wayfinding were apparent, standing tall at the helm as their ships emerged from the storm, in some cases stronger and more seaworthy.

But sometimes, captains get it wrong. Sometimes their intuitive pattern recognition malfunctions.

The Sinking of the El Faro: Intuition Bias at Its Most Deadly

"It's time to come this way!" Those were the last words spoken by Captain Michael Davidson as he yelled from the navigation bridge of *El Faro* before it was swallowed by the sea.

The recovered recorder of the 791-foot cargo ship revealed the tragic story of one of the worst US maritime disasters. On October 1, 2015, El Faro sailed into the eyewall of Hurricane Joaquin. Captain Davidson, a respected American merchant captain, with a reputation for being unusually competent, structured, organized, and also known as a "stickler for safety," instead followed his knotted intuition into the depths of the deep blue sea.

Here's the backstory. Three years earlier, Davidson, with a mission to sail a ship down the Chesapeake from one port to another, refused to set sail when the surveyor determined the steering gear to be unreliable. The decision cost him his job. Far worse was the resulting damage to his confidence and sense of security. Fast forward, Davidson earned his way to the helm of an old "rustbucket," the El Faro, earning the highest marks for his years of captaining the ship. With the hope of soon commanding one of the company's new ships and tainted by the outcome of his "safe" decision that cost him his earlier job, Davidson's intuition bias and other colluding mind knots hijacked his good sense.

Aware that a tropical depression in the Atlantic had intensified into Tropical Storm Joaquin, Davidson considered two possible routes. One would take the ship around a string of wave-breaking islands providing some cover from the storm, though it would have added six hours to the journey. Influenced by his "gut," the route Davidson chose was the "straight shot," avoiding the additional six hours at sea, reasoning his superiors would be pleased by his completing his San Juan mission on time.

Shortly after the ship set sail, Joaquin became a Category 1 hurricane. Evidence showed the storm was intensifying. Erring on the side of caution, Davidson's chief mate suggested adjusting the route immediately. Instead, Davidson chose to wait for additional information, though when it arrived, it was at least twelve hours old due to a software glitch.

As the sun rose the next morning, Davidson pointed out the bright red sky in the distance. You probably know the saying, "Red sky at night, sailors delight. Red sky in morning, sailors take warning." Knowing this was a clear warning sign, Davidson dismissed the threatening sky commenting, "Ship's solid." The next storm report confirmed the storm was moving fast and they were on a collision course with Joaquin.

Conditions were changing for the worse, and another weather report was delivered confirming the ship was frighteningly on course to meet with the eye of the storm. The third mate who was monitoring the weather broadcasts continued to express strong concern about the reported power of the storm and warned his ship mates, "We can't outrun it....it's more powerful than we thought." Yet, Davidson had no reaction.

The National Hurricane Center delivered an updated report that night showing the storm had intensified and was officially registered as a Category 3. With winds projected to be 126 mph with gusts to 155, the crew notified Davidson and recommended they follow the escape route that the third mate had plotted. Instead, Davidson dismissed the plan, *feeling* the storm would progress more slowly.

Only hours later, the ship was pitching violently, rolling, and pounding. The second mate called Davidson to again propose an escape route. Captain Davidson rejected her suggestion and went back to sleep.

Entering a squall, conditions deteriorated, and the ship was under tremendous stress including a loss of electrical connections. Below the main deck, water washed in through the sides. Despite waves pounding the vessel and the steering alarm sounding, Davidson continued to downplay the storm, announcing, "There's nothing bad about this ride...I was sleeping like a baby." Reality showed otherwise, though. Sea conditions were atrocious. Fighting mountainous waves, Davidson attempted to turn the ship to shift the direction of the winds on the vessel. The ship continued to list severely and then its propulsion stopped.

Davidson's intuition bias convinced him he would prevail—until reality took over. As the night's darkness lifted, the catastrophic circumstances were clear. Yet Davidson, relying on his *sense*, announced, "Right now we're on the back side of it." His gut was wrong. They were in the northern eyewall and Joaquin was intensifying into a Category 4 hurricane.

With the ship continuing to deteriorate, including the loss of the main engine, Davidson eventually reached out to the home office, and reported his latitude and longitude and said, "Just wanted to give you a heads-up before I push that button." He was referring to the emergency distress signal.

El Faro was fighting against thirty- to forty-foot waves slamming over the ship while listing at a very steep fifteen degrees.

Davidson's superior assured him he would inform the Coast Guard.

Davidson repeated, "I wanna push that button...I just wanted to give you the courtesy so you wouldn't be blindsided by it... Everybody's safe right now. We're in survival mode now."

His superior replied, "You do your thing, Captain." That was the last communication with the ship before it sank.

When it really counted, Davidson's "good" intuition should have been screaming at him. Instead, it proved to be his gnarl, not his gift.

The Overconfidence Bias

Overconfidence amplifies the negative effects of intuition, further pushing intuitive captains toward an instinctual option, confidently believing it to be superior to any other non-intuitive choice, even when both choices seem valid.

This mind knot creates big waves for intuitive captains, intensifying the strength of their intuition and diminishing their odds of taking a logical path to reasoning in decision-making. Overconfidence makes it easy for captains to trust their gut, avoiding the cognitive load of logical analysis, which these captains naturally avoid.

So how do we recognize unreliable intuition that is bolstered by an overconfidence mind knot? A simple sign is to ask, do I have a good explanation for my confidence? If the answer is no, there is usually trouble ahead.

The Well-Traveled Road Effect

Google acquired Android in 2005, and years later, Bill Gates admitted his "greatest mistake ever was whatever mismanagement he engaged in that caused Microsoft not to be where Android is." He recognized Android to be the standard non-Apple phone platform and "that was a natural thing for Microsoft to win." He went on to say, "There's room for exactly one non-Apple operating system and what's that worth? $400 billion that would be transferred from company G to company M."

The "mismanagement" to which Gates referred was likely due to his intuition failing him, in combination with missing signals as a result of staying in the familiar lane of his well-traveled Microsoft journey. This is exactly what happens when companies become too comfortable with the familiar routes they travel. The Well-Traveled Road Effect is a bias that explains why "travelers" either overestimate or underestimate the time it will take for a particular journey because of their familiarity with the route. But familiarity causes other problems beyond a miscalculation of timing.

Route familiarity can cause companies to underestimate the importance of time to market, or to overlook new signals and routes because staying in a familiar lane makes it easy to miss changes and opportunities along the way.

Satya Nadella, named CEO of Microsoft in 2014, intuitively recognized the danger in the *comfort* of remaining on Microsoft's "well-traveled" route, openly acknowledging the risk of missing innovation and market opportunities. This is an all-too-common reality for maturing or well-matured businesses. It's like repeatedly driving down the same familiar roads on autopilot. We've all been there.

Think of a time when you comfortably traveled a familiar route and zoned out, missing a turn or an exit. Perhaps you encountered a detour that threw you off, causing you to arrive late, completely missing the boat.

Similarly, relying on a record of past performance can trigger a default to cruise control, with similar risk of missing signals that could inform better choices of speed, timing, or routes to the destination.

The Past Performance Mind Knot

In most hiring situations, there is a bias toward past performance.

In fact, past performance continues to be a favored signal for future performance, even though previous experience rarely aligns as expected with the actual situation or mission in question. Now, I'm not saying experience doesn't matter. I am saying the *right* experience matters—experience that matches the context and reality of the mission and situation at hand.

Past performance and well-traveled routes are part of the patterns and information that live in our personal repositories, helping to inform our intuition. But when we anchor on select experiences or routes without considering new realities or shifts in context and situation—well, that's when intuition is certain to be a gnarl instead of a gift.

While intuition references past experience and performance, more importantly it zigzags through multiple dimensions of information stored in our personal repository. This perceptive mind knot also scans for relevant patterns from accretive learning and knowledge, enabling connections that apply to the reality of a current situation.

Firmly footed on the captain's bridge, so to speak, intuition is forward-facing while unconsciously tapping into an integrated network of non-specific knowledge, including signals accumulated from the past to inform a new journey ahead. When intuition and past performance mind knots collide, an overreliance on the past to inform the future can steer the ship, resulting in a risky mission with the promise of a limited outcome.

The Availability Bias and the "Playbook Approach"

Availability bias, also rearview focused, further complicates Captains of Wayfinding's judgment. Urging recall of experiences that are memorable, *easily available*, and often emotionally charged, the availability mind knot can surface easy-to-recall experiences whether they are applicable to the current situation or not. Those experiences are then wrongly considered as relevant, guiding present decisions that bear little resemblance to the *available* referenced experience. At the same time, important experiences that are less memorable, and laced with less emotion, are not easily recollected, and therefore left out of the equation.

Here's the twist. While experience recall does not ensure appropriateness to a situation, an available memory may nevertheless serve as a key informant to intuition, dangerously rigging judgment and decisions to an unsuitable recollection and thus, irrational reasoning or "garbage in, garbage out."

Similarly, representativeness is a common cognitive bias that also maroons good intuition. It inclines leaders to reference similar experiences, assuming there is a correlation between the situations and their *outcomes*. This logic loop launches captains into a "playbook" execution approach, expecting that what worked in the past will work in the present—even when context, situation, and circumstances don't actually align.

Science shows, in leadership where performance and success are well recognized, captains tend to trust their experiences and memories of their past performance, making them more susceptible to this web of cognitive coils—past performance, availability, and representativeness mind knots—each amplifying intuition bias.

The Knotty Truth

"Good analysis in the hands of managers who have good judgment won't naturally yield good decisions."

—C. JACKSON GRAYSON,

AMERICAN BUSINESS: A TWO-MINUTE WARNING

This quote by Grayson gets right to the core problem: *mind knots*, hijackers of good thinking and reasoned decision-making. His work underscored the idea that while analysis provides valuable data and insights, the ability to make sound decisions ultimately depends on the judgment of the managers and leaders handling that analysis.

While we want to believe we are clear thinkers and rational decision-makers, our best intentions and efforts are compromised more often than we would care to admit. Mind knots explain why, to the contrary, many decisions at all levels of management and leadership—whether from the captain's bridge, the boardroom, or the back office—so often yield poor outcomes, even when informed by the best analysis possible.

It's common for leaders to credit their success to their "business savvy" and good intuition. Yet, as we have seen, intuition bias can get in the way of business sense and acumen.

Business savvy, like intuition, is not easily measured, though it remains high on the list of requirements in most leadership mandates. When I've asked clients to describe what "business savvy" means to them, definitions are a bit all over the place. Some say, "A nose for business," or, "Someone who just gets it." Others say, "A leader with a good business sense and a good gut."

While all of these comments are valid, there are two key considerations that are egregiously overlooked: situational sense and cognitive biases. And both impact clear eyes, clear thinking, and sound judgment.

At the end of the day, there are really two key factors to consider in making judgments, decisions, and choices: What we know, and how we rationalize it.

The process of rationalizing is exactly where biases get in our way. Unless we know and understand the knots that hijack our minds, we can't begin to manage them. Instead, our biases will most certainly tangle and taint the way we rationalize...*everything*.

So how can leaders manage their intuition bias for good outcomes? Let's take a look.

NAVIGATION KNOTS AND TACKS

The Captain's Compass for Captains of Wayfinding can provide directional insights to help these leaders navigate the perils of intuition bias. The Compass highlights directional biases that will either hinder or help these leaders.

The East Cardinal Point: Magnifying Mind Knots

The Well-Traveled Road Effect

The well-traveled road bias pertains to the perception of *familiarity*, and how it impacts our judgment, often of time and distance, though in leadership this mind knot has broader implications.

Familiarity reduces the cognitive load of processing the environment. The well-traveled road bias played a role in gnarled intuition both in the example of Microsoft missing their Android opportunity, and Captain Davidson's grave misjudgment of Hurricane Joaquin. In addition to missing good intuition signals, both were led by their well-traveled experiences, which presided over the reality of current conditions in their respective environments, blinding them to a potential course correction to a better outcome.

The Intuition Bias

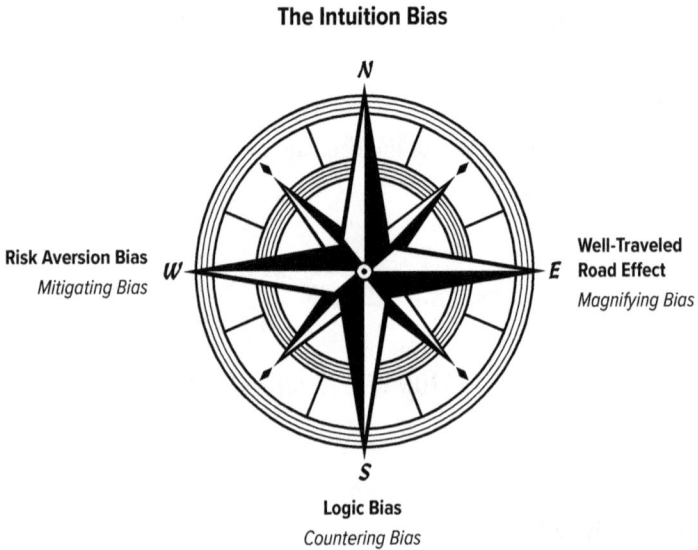

The Captain's Compass: Captains of Wayfinding

Whether we consider depth and expertise in a particular area or past performance within a particular lane, familiarity invites danger. Common consequences of familiarity in leadership include underestimating the complexity or duration of initiatives, resistance to change, and not considering new routes to problem-solving. It can also lead to an empathy gap that causes leaders to ignore others who don't share the same familiarity with a situation; when this occurs, they may fail to provide necessary explanations and context when communicating. A lack of vigilance is another hitch to familiarity, manifesting in unrecognized or unanticipated challenges or opportunities.

While experience and familiarity are invaluable in leadership, both introduce serious biases, and the well-traveled road effect mind knot is one of them.

The West Cardinal Point: Mitigating Mind Knot

Risk Aversion Bias

Captains of Wayfinding easily *accept* risks that come along with their feelings-based approach to decision-making. Risk Aversion bias, the inclination to *avoid* risk, can be an effective strategy for mitigating a wayward intuition bias.

Ram Charan, author of *The Attacker's Advantage: Turning Uncertainty into Breakthrough Opportunities*, suggests risk-takers are "doers who take risks based partly on fact, and partly on their imagination about what could happen when those forces combine in what others might later call a convergence." He refers to risk-takers as "catalysts" to the convergence of breakthroughs. You know the saying—no risk, no reward.

Risk-averse leaders prefer safe play. They have a low tolerance for uncertainty even when the potential upside of the outcome is greater than its potential loss. On the other hand, intuition bias steers toward uncertainty and risk based on a *sense* of a greater upside than loss.

On its own, risk aversion prevents breakthroughs, innovation, and even moderate progress across companies because it favors being safe over being risky. However, this bias can be an effective strategy for wayfinding leaders who often tilt the ship with risk. Adopting tacks associated with averting headwinds can mitigate the risk associated with a purely intuitive choice.

The South Cardinal Point: Countering Mind Knot

The Logic Bias

Logic is associated with "principled" reasoning. It offers *structured* cognitive guidance. Logic can guide the meaningful connection between information, insight, and intuition, ensuring associations are validly integrated.

Because logical thinking is the opposite of intuitive thinking, it represents a counter-approach, taming intuition bias. In contrast to intuition, logic pursues a linear, conscious, and methodical approach to collecting and structuring relevant data to arrive at meaningful associations for a "logical" conclusion.

On its own, a logic mind knot would devalue intuition. But when logical thinking and intuitive thinking work in collaboration, the result is improved reasoning, even when intuition is steering the ship.

NAVIGATING INTUITION BIAS

Questions – Know your knots

- Have my intuitive decisions consistently led to positive outcomes, or have there been instances where they have resulted in errors or setbacks?
- Do I use intuition as a starting point to generate hypotheses that are then tested with evidence, or do I rely solely on intuition without further examination?

- Do I strike a balance between trusting my intuition and conducting objective analysis, depending on the nature of the decision?

Tacking Techniques

- Identify a fact-based accountability partner to challenge "intuitive" ideas.
- Seek diverse perspectives from team members and experts outside your inner circle and encourage dissenting opinions by inviting feedback and modeling open-mindedness.
- Consider additional hypotheses to avoid jumping to conclusions. Practice questioning and critical thinking to challenge assumptions.
- Use analysis to narrow down options and intuition to choose the best one.
- Anticipate the outcome of a failed intuition-driven decision and consider how logic could have changed the outcome.
- Adopt a decision-making framework that infuses data and empirical evidence into the process to avoid the sway of preconceptions and intuition bias.

THE RATIONAL SOLUTION

Leaders with a tighter intuitive knot will trust their gut over heeding a more logical approach to decisions. And leaders who are bound to logic will rely on data-driven reasoning over what their intuition may be telling them. Good intuition is important in leadership. So, whether in "thinkers" or "feelers," the question is, can intuition be improved?

The answer is yes—to some degree.

Now, that might be surprising. But in a way, intuition is earned. For intuition to be effective, one must acknowledge the feeling and accept the invitation to the guidance it offers. Honoring our intuition, and prudently letting it guide us, helps us to stretch our intuitive muscle. Integrating intuitive whispers with data and structured thinking will strengthen the power of good intuition, while mitigating the danger of the intuition mind knot.

Another part of what makes intuition effective is the unconscious accumulation, storage, and effective retrieval of *tacit* knowledge.

Here's the catch. The facet of intuitive ability that enables unconscious consumption and storage of complex information differs from person to person. Therefore, experience on its own is not an indicator of intuitive ability. Rather, it's the capacity for *implicit* learning or absorbing complex information *without knowing it* that supports the accumulation of tacit knowledge—the foundation of intuition.

We all have differing degrees of tacit knowledge stored in our personal repository against which current impressions and perceptions are matched, making our *wisdom* personal and accretive. Highly intuitive people have a strong capacity for tacit knowledge.

Further, critical thinking can be learned, improving the effectiveness of intuition. How? By engaging in deliberate ways to broaden thinking, including: seeking diverse perspectives; practicing and adopting logical approaches to collecting, organizing, and analyzing data; challenging personal assumptions; and considering alternatives, especially when the stakes are high. These are all valid ways to improve critical thinking.

Intuition, Analysis, and Guiding Principles

In her study "Lessons from 'Good Minds': How CEOs use Intuition, Analysis and Guiding Principles to Make Strategic Decisions," researcher Jaana Woiceshyn examined how successful executives managed complex decisions. She established that decision-makers in complex situations and under time pressure will bypass deliberate, rational analysis, and instead depend on their intuition or cognitive shortcuts, referred to as "scripts and schemas."

Woiceshyn examined the role of intuition and cognitive tools in effective strategic decision-making, presenting a model that integrates intuition *and* rational analysis.

The study included CEOs who were well-recognized for their decision-making success, as well as CEOs recognized for unsuccessful decisions. All the captains in her study had long tenure in the same industry, which controlled for industry-related nuances. Woiceshyn noted that experience was not the only factor affecting the quantity and quality of intuition.

Her findings showed the effective CEOs were successful not by substituting intuition for rational analysis, but by combining intuition and logic in iterative processes, which she referred to as "integration by essentials," "principles," and "spiraling." The study focused on the decision-making *processes* of these CEOs, with particular attention to processing differences between the "good outcome" and "bad outcome" CEOs.

Let's first dive into the meaning of *essentials, principles,* and *spiraling,* the processes attributed to the CEOs who were effective in achieving good outcomes.

Integration by Essentials, Principles, and Spiraling

Integration by essentials (IBE) "governs intuitive (subconscious) storage and retrieval of all the relevant knowledge bearing on a decision." *Principles* are derived from relevant knowledge and experience that is stored as meaningful statements or short-cuts. And *spiraling* describes "the rapid evaluation of the decision alternatives. It involves zooming in on the most feasible alternative with the help of identified principles, and then using the principles to test and adjust the decision before committing to it."

The study revealed, "When intuition does not provide knowledge integrated by *essentials,* or relevant information, rational evaluation is not possible, and decision making is hampered." It showed that the retrieval process of the less effective CEOs was based on vague associations and *feelings,* instead of "essentials."

Principles, Not Scripts

Instead of relying on routine "scripts," the effective CEOs asked many questions to get to the facts to integrate into their existing knowledge. They demonstrated a strong desire for objectivity and routinely sought outside expert opinions from consultants, board members, and investment bankers to guard against any possible bias. They also led teams with diverse backgrounds and opinions, and one of the CEOs in the success group intentionally "embraced the skeptics" within the company.

In combination with their intuition, the successful CEOs employed logical tactics and disciplined thinking. They constantly assessed the quality of information they considered, and they avoided committing to any one idea too soon without seeking evidence.

Principles condense vast amounts of knowledge and accumulated experience into simple and meaningful statements that are easy to hold onto and retrieve to aid in decision-making. Woiceshyn suggests the dominant view is that decision-makers are guided by their "knowledge structures" or cognitive filters including heuristics, scripts, or schemas, *instead of principles*.

So, "over time, knowledge structures become cognitive shortcuts, allowing for quick behavioral responses in familiar situations, based on a script developed from previous experience," instead of a meaningful principle.

The problem is that scripts tend to be inflexible and can become "decision traps." This is exactly what we saw in the story of Captain Davidson in the *El Faro* story.

Woiceshyn also found that *principles* protected the CEOs against other cognitive knots common to a decision-making process, including framing, overconfidence, and escalating commitment. Each of these cognitive kinks compels leaders to follow one another's conclusions blindly, evading facts, or pretending that data and facts are other than what they are.

Let's consider the Honesty Principle, for example, which "guides one not to fake reality in order to gain a value." The effective CEOs in the study "regarded honesty as a general principle: it guided their thinking and conduct constantly." Woiceshyn points out honesty was a key principle because "Honesty emphasizes rejection of that which is unreal—and thus helps keep one's thinking focused on facts and is thereby effective."

Masters of Instinct and Logic Spiraling

The difference between the effective CEOs and the less effective CEOs was notable. The less effective CEOs recognized the scenario as familiar. However, this was merely by association, such as, "I have seen a company do something similar before." They failed to identify essential similarities *or* differences between the current situation and their previous experiences, and thus were unable to quickly dismiss any of the alternatives. They did not effectively reference their tacit knowledge or personal wisdom, nor were they processing the facts of the situation.

The effective CEOs were very aware of their own decision-making approach and potential bias, and they were comfortable thinking out loud about how they would handle the situation. Many openly walked through their decision steps and approach, referring to principles they used in reaching their decision. The less effective CEOs were not as self-aware.

In summary, this study revealed the decision-making process of the effective CEOs showed clear evidence of integrating intuition and rational analysis. They translated their knowledge into concepts and principles versus scripts, enabling them to apply their "abstract condensations" of knowledge and experience to multiple concrete decision situations.

These CEOs made decisions by *spiraling* through iterative decision loops, aided by their principles that allowed fast and effective decision-making without omitting any relevant information. These principles enabled them to see and understand what was essential in any given situation, and to make good use of their intuition.

The Captain's Bridge: Where Mental Agility Matters

On a ship, the bridge is the hub for judgment and decisions. It is where situations are assessed, approaches are considered, judgment is levied, and decisions are made.

It's where complexity is processed, organized, and translated into strategies and action. And, in the best of situations, it's where intuition intersects with logic, resulting in sound and savvy decisions, and consequently, good outcomes.

Mental agility matters, and it relies on integrative thinking. The ability to embrace intuition while simultaneously leveraging the discipline of logical information processing is key to effectively managing complexity, with clear connections, circumstances, and conclusions. Mastering mental agility in this case means thinking neither only intuitively nor only linearly. Rather, it is the ability to manage and leverage the differences in both thinking protocols. It is not dissimilar to contradictory thinking.

Jerry Fletcher and Kelle Olwyer, authors of *Paradoxical Thinking: How to Profit from Your Contradictions*, propose a method of leveraging contradictory characteristics to achieve outstanding performance. The authors argue that, where performance is optimal, paradoxical thinking is always in play. It should come as no surprise, then, that a fixed mindset or way of thinking, whether intuitive or logical, is like being stuck in a brain bind. It limits thinking and possibilities and reduces choices.

Captains of Wayfinding who develop the mental agility to leverage their intuition and savvy, striking connections between personal wisdom, situation sense, real-time signals, and circumstances, along with logical processing practices, prove to be the captains who achieve remarkable growth and outcomes in their personal and business journeys. The savviest Captains of Wayfinding have the mental agility to become the skilled skippers of integrative thinking.

Integrative Thinking

Integrative thinkers welcome complexity in decision-making and problem-solving because they "know" that's where the best answers come from. Most importantly, integrative thinkers can hold all components of a problem or decision suspended in their minds at once, resulting in better options, solutions, and outcomes.

Roger L. Martin, author of *The Opposable Mind* and a *Harvard Business Review* article, "How Successful Leaders Think," maintains that it's not superior strategy or faultless execution that define most exceptional leaders. Rather, it's the discipline of integrative thinking. Unlike conventional thinkers, these savvy leaders are discerning, seeing the full architecture of the problem, how all pieces fit together, and how one decision will affect another.

Zigzagging and Integrating

Unlike logical thinking, which moves linearly, intuitive thinking is far from sequential. Rather, it moves from side to side – it zigzags. Zigzagging enables these captains to unconsciously process, examine, and quickly integrate multiple ideas.

In William Manchester's biography of Winston Churchill, noted as one of the greatest intuitive leaders of all time, the author writes about Churchill's intuitive mind. "The statesman was a notoriously poor student academically. But...he had a zig-zag lightning of the brain."

In his own words, Churchill revealed his natural intuitive and integrative thinking ability, and his understanding of the value of logical reasoning, by saying, "No idea is so outlandish that it should not be considered with a searching, but at the same time a steady eye."

Having the mental agility to combine both intuitive and logical processing is a key differentiator in leadership strength and effectiveness. Ram Charan, world-renowned business advisor, speaker, and author of many business and leadership books, including *Leaders at all Levels* and *What the CEO Wants You to Know*, claims superior CEOs use their business acumen "to test the logic of their priorities and the path on which they are setting the business....These are the people who intuitively understand the connections between customers, profits, money they borrow, and money they take in." Charan adds that the leader needs greater mental breadth and depth to make the connections between the complexities of the outside world and intricacies of moneymaking specific to the business.

The evidence is overwhelming. Intuition is a gift when it is properly supported and empowered with logic and reasoning. So, let's put a name to this approach. I'll call it the Sound and Savvy Model.

The Sound and Savvy Model: The Rational Way Forward

The Sound and Savvy Model provides a framework for *intuitive intelligence* by blending the "irrationality" of intuition bias with the rationality of logic, not simply to discipline intuition, but to empower it.

The model guides captains and their organizations to embrace the tension of intuition and logic, leveraging both in equal strength and merit, though operating in contradiction to each other. It is the healthy tension between these two contradictory thinking styles that proves to be the winning strategy for bridging intuition and logical thinking. A sound and savvy thinking process is far superior to either sound or savvy thinking independently.

THE BOTTOM LINE: ALL HANDS ON DECK

The leader sets the tone for the organization, and with a Wayfinding Captain at the helm, intuition is likely to rule the course, barring intervention.

The goal is not only to avoid decision errors but to optimize opportunities and outcomes. This agile framework provides guidance for Captains of Wayfinding and their organizations to improve decision-making and optimize outcomes, honoring the gift of intuition with the discipline of logical reasoning.

The Sound and Savvy Mission Objectives

- Merge subconscious intelligence with conscious intelligence in decision-processing—at the helm and across the organization.
- Harness the positive force of intuition by empowering it with logic.

The Strategy Equation

Intuition Bias + Logic Bias =
The Sound and Savvy Model

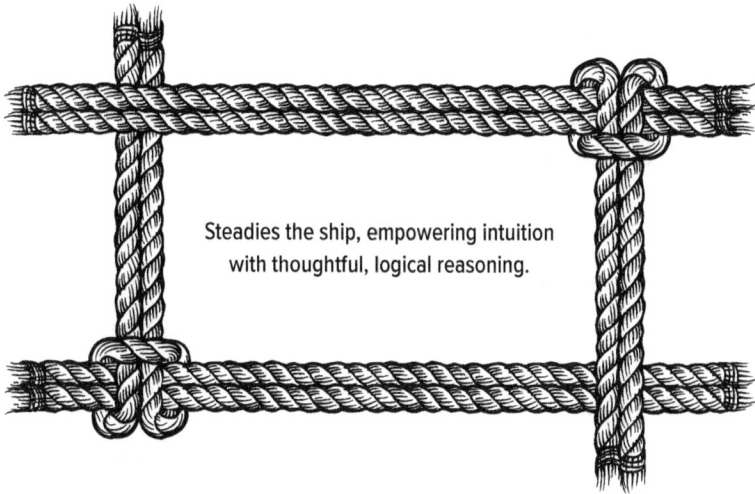

Steadies the ship, empowering intuition
with thoughtful, logical reasoning.

Strategic Maneuvers and Organizational Guidance:
The Sound and Savvy Model

The critical point is to instill the cross-functional accountability required to influence and affect enterprise-wide, systemic, and sustainable behavioral change, integrating the power of intuition *and* logical reasoning.

While some of the suggestions below may not fit your situation, the idea is to consider the practices and leverage or modify them to a version that makes sense for your organization.

The Captain

- Cultivate self-awareness and regularly reflect on your own thinking, judgment, and decision processes to identify instances where intuition bias may be at play.
- Emphasize the organizational risk of operating as an "intuitive" culture, drawing attention to the potential

negative impact of decisions based on intuitive, unevidenced, or incomplete information. Define and communicate the organization's risk tolerance levels.

- Prioritize adopting a decision process that harnesses the value drivers of intuition and the value drivers of logic, for good judgment and decision-making. Incorporate agile methodologies including Scrum-like decision analysis sessions where teams critically evaluate and challenge intuitive-leaning decisions, highlighting potential risks and vulnerabilities.
- For new change initiatives, pair an intuitive thinker with an analytical thinker to co-lead the initiative, ensuring both have eyes on the horizon.
- Practice integrative thinking: embrace intuition and logical processing while considering the full architecture of a problem, how all pieces fit together, and how one decision will affect another over time, known as second-order thinking.
- Identify common reasoning fallacies and mental anchors in group decision-making instances to prevent subconscious undertows from drowning good decisions.

The Crew—Leadership Team

- Support and leverage the captain's natural ability for fast and efficient decision-making by providing cover with timely data and analysis.
- Encourage team members to recognize the propensity of intuition bias and its influence on decisions they make and actions they take.

- Provide decision support tools and resources that guide leaders and employees through logical analysis and risk assessment processes.
- Implement a practice of documenting decisions, including the intuitive and evidence-based reasoning that led to them, continuously improving the decision process.

People Processes

- Develop an organization-wide intuition-bias awareness program. Provide strategies to harness the *savvy* power of intuition through *sound* information processing and evidence-based decision-making. Emphasize the value of combining intuitive and analytical thinking while highlighting the merits of each and the power of combining both.
- Provide training programs focused on intuition bias, critical and integrative thinking, and risk management.
- Plan a leadership team off-site training event designed to illustrate the downside to unmanaged intuition and logic biases, while also highlighting the importance of risk management and integrative thinking. Form two teams representing self-identified intuitive-leaning and analytical-leaning decision makers to engage in a role-play decision process. Have each team argue a decision from the perspective of the other, enabling awareness of the value and challenges associated with both intuition bias and logic bias.
- Support hiring managers with behavioral interviewing techniques and objective assessment tools to assess indicators of intuitive and logical thinking propensities.

Financial Considerations

- Implement a peer review practice for financial decisions and include third-party independent reviewers to ensure impulsive intuitive decisions are squared against logical reasoning and facts.
- Promote the use of cost-benefit analysis and similar quantitative techniques to objectively assess the potential risks and rewards of options.
- Assign members of the finance team to participate in functional project decision processes, to manage risk associated with intuitive-leaning initiatives by strengthening analytical thinking within the decision process.

Commercial Considerations

- Prioritize data-driven decision-making in commercial strategies, including the collection and analysis of market data and competitor analysis.
- Form collaborative partnerships in sales and marketing, pairing intuitive executives with analytical counterparts to ensure commercial endeavors are both sound and savvy.
- Use an objective approach when evaluating potential opportunities or strategies by asking questions such as "Will this solution offer us a competitive advantage?" or "Could this lead to increased revenues?" Ask *how* and *why* after both questions and support with data.
- Rely on evidence in addition to "gut feeling" when evaluating new business. Utilize analytical tools to detect

emerging patterns in customer behavior and market trends that may not be easily recognized through simple observation or human judgment.

Board Considerations

- Ensure the captain's intuitive strength is empowered and supported, while holding the captain accountable to a strong reasoning process backed by valid data.
- Require a "Checks & Balances" process to mitigate intuition-leaning decisions.
- Promote cognitive diversity on the board and leadership team to reduce the risk of intuitive-driven governance.

Five Questions to Identify Indicators of Intuition Bias

1. How confident are you in making decisions without looking at data?
2. Describe a decision that, in hindsight, you wish you'd approached differently. Did you rely on your gut feeling? What would you change about how you made that decision?
3. Have you experienced a situation where an intuitive decision caused unexpected results? What would you have done to improve the situation and outcome?
4. Are there times when you feel reluctant to objectively evaluate the evidence before making a decision?
5. How do you validate your intuitive judgments? Have there been instances where team members or colleagues have challenged your gut feelings?

TAKEAWAYS: TYING IT ALL TOGETHER

Captains of Wayfinding

Wayfinding captains are prominent holders of intuition bias. They have a unique "Spidey Sense" that sets them apart from others, distinguishing them as fast-thinking and savvy leaders.

They are integrative and zigzag thinkers, referencing their personal knowledge repository to guide decisions and actions. "Intuitive Smarts" and personal wisdom are key characteristics of these captains. While they reference past impressions, they think and act in the present to affect the future.

The Intuition Bias

This bias references past experiences, patterns, and perceptions to inform present decisions and initiatives. Intuition is a double-edged sword for Captains of Wayfinding. It is both their gift and their gnarl.

Intuition is a clear strength in time-sensitive situations when fast thinking is required. The intuition mind knot overemphasizes instinct happening in the present over time-consuming perspective gathering and relevance analysis of things that happened in the past.

This mind knot often invokes emotion, which can alienate rational thinking and can take these captains and their ships down when unmanaged.

The Rational Solution: The Sound and Savvy Model

This model is a rational way forward for Captains of Wayfinding. It can be transformative for these captains and the organizations they lead, offering them the opportunity to elevate their savvy "smarts" to rational wisdom by mentally managing their intuitive strength alongside logical thinking.

This framework requires agile thinking—not by replacing intuition with logic, but rather employing both at the same time using integrative thinking and logical reasoning.

The Sound and Savvy model helps these captains navigate from being intuitive wayfinding leaders to becoming intelligent intuitive captains.

NINE

THE PLANNING BIAS

"Success is so much easier to imagine than failure. There is often only one correct outcome we hope to achieve, yet countless ways for the plan to go haywire."

—DANIEL KAHNEMAN

THE PLANNING FALLACY BIAS

PSYCHOLOGISTS DANIEL KAHNEMAN AND THE LATE Amos Tversky brought the phenomenon of the planning fallacy to light in 1979. Their research revealed that this optimistically skewed bias is the reason why we so often fail in our planning. Basically, this mind knot highlights our tendency to underestimate important planning factors, including time, costs, and risks involved in an initiative, while at the same time prompting us to overestimate the initiative's benefits and positive outcomes.

While planning is essential and central to every organization, the planning bias presents one of the biggest threats to success because it creates *optimistic prediction inaccuracies* across multiple planning principles, including scope, resources, and timing.

Timing, a key principle of planning, is one of the areas most affected by this mind knot.

For instance, information overload, often a reality in planning, inevitably creates delays in processing and analyzing data. Then, due to the optimistic undercurrent of this mind knot, estimations of timing and resources needed to complete the initiative are typically underestimated, setting the plan off course. Further, long-term project plans with far-reaching deadlines create *abstraction*, making planning and predicting an even greater challenge to unravel.

Kahneman and Tversky also noted that we tend to think we are more capable than we actually are and that we know more than we really do. They referred to this phenomenon as taking the "inside view," which causes us to imagine events will unfold exactly as we think they will.

In fact, things almost never unfold as we imagine they will. Inevitably, the *best plan* is rife with unexpected interruptions, obstacles, and delays. Our subjective estimations and predictions are mostly unrealistic and incorrect due to optimism and overconfidence. And our propensity to hitch our plan to memories or blueprints from *familiar* experiences that seem similar in some way, though actually not, distorts our predictions even more.

Planning is a cornerstone in business intended to enable *safe* passage to a future state, and it can provide us with a false sense of control. Yet, without planning, businesses would operate reactively, rather than proactively—ultimately going adrift. But even with planning, the force of the planning fallacy bias puts missions at risk.

The planning fallacy mind knot accounts for failed plans, projects, products, and businesses in record numbers. For instance, it has been calculated that 80 percent of start-ups fail to achieve initial market predictions, largely due to this mind knot.

As experts Kahneman and Tversky discovered in their work, planning fallacy bias hijacks the integrity of effective planning, causing us to fail more than we succeed in planning, executing, and achieving outcomes on time, on budget, or even at all.

CAPTAINS OF OCEAN BOILING

Now, what exactly do I mean by "ocean boiling"?

The phrase "to boil the ocean" refers to the concept of making things more complicated than they need to be. In trying to accomplish something that is overly ambitious, unfocused, or a massive undertaking, *boiling the ocean* can be a typical default.

In business, a planner's quest is to chart a course toward a future that is predicted, yet uncertain. Planners and forecasters must draw upon the most relevant information, data, and analysis to make critical predictions for the business mission. One must consider strategy, timing, resource planning, capital investment, and many other factors, all of which will affect the execution of their plan.

Often, planning can take on a life of its own—sometimes due to a captain's aversion to risk. Anchoring in the harbor of risk aversion usually manifests in excessive planning and pointless *ocean boiling*.

Captains of Ocean Boiling, nobly aiming to validate their work and avoid risk, will submerge themselves in fact-finding and analysis, sometimes well beyond their objective's scope and focus.

Though risk-averse by nature and well-intentioned, these captains aim to deliver sturdy navigation to the future state for which they are planning. They are inherently curious, conscientious, and cautious, predisposing them to dive deep to confirm their plan.

Here's the problem. Over-researched, overprocessed, and overanalyzed plans cause delays in execution, missed deadlines, unachieved outcomes, and even missed opportunities. The unintended consequences of ocean boiling can sabotage the very outcome the plan is being designed to deliver—the execution and timeliness of a smooth sail to a future state.

Prediction, Ideals, and Flexibility

Accurate predictions of timing are a significant challenge for planning leaders, especially those who are deep divers or prone to "scope creep" or prioritization challenges. Despite the optimistic undercurrent of this mind knot, planning leaders are charged with preparing for uncertainty, including managing and mitigating risk. In their aim for accuracy, they can sometimes plunge too deep, caught in an endless spiral of perfectionism.

Captains of Ocean Boiling often tie themselves to an *ideal* scenario, where everything goes according to plan, and nothing goes wrong. Hitched to this ideal, these captains can find themselves blindly immersed in their diving efforts, overlooking market realities and other important factors above the waterline. Anchored to their ideal plan, they can unknowingly discount the very sensitive relationship between timing and opportunity. Under the influence of the planning bias, Captains of Ocean Boiling may also ignore another important principle of planning—flexibility.

These leaders are often domain experts. Despite their expertise, they are driven to latch on to as much data as possible to confirm their beliefs, often convincing themselves they have greater power to influence the future than they actually do.

Now you might be thinking, if truly experts, they would surely be sensitive to situational realities and factors that could affect their planning initiatives, wouldn't they? So why in the world would they fall into the whirlpool of ocean boiling and succumb to the planning fallacy's deceptive errors? Certainly, these expert planning captains would possess the experience and wisdom required to save themselves from overly optimistic predictions. Right?

Wrong.

Unable to predict the future with certainty or to control the unknown, Captains of Ocean Boiling easily veer off course due to residual effects of their aversion to risk *and* the optimistic undertow of the planning fallacy—both swaying them toward inaccurate estimations of timing and resources.

Captains of Ocean Boiling are the "over and under" captains: over on the preparing and ideal projections, and under on predictions of time, resources, budget, challenges, and risks.

Here's the thing. A plan is only good when the value of its intended outcome is greater than the cost associated with its planning. Ocean boiling destroys planning's return on investment (ROI).

A Confirming Colluder to Planning Bias

Confirmation Bias

Confirmation bias guides Captains of Ocean Boiling to interpret information in a way that supports and *confirms* their belief in their plan. Harboring a need to be right, these captains will selectively pay attention to data that aligns with their ideas and plan, dismissing information that doesn't support it.

Here's the twist. Despite all the deep diving and ocean boiling they may do in search of information to inform a strategic and sturdy plan, this confirmation mind knot teases and tempts these captains to hitch onto only the information and data that confirm their personal thinking and plan preference—increasing instead of decreasing risk.

The Evolution of Planning

"The plan of action is at one and the same time, the result envisaged, the line of action to be followed, the stages to go through, and the methods to use."
—HENRI FAYOL, FRENCH MANAGEMENT
THEORIST AND INDUSTRIALIST

Some would say the genesis of modern industrial planning began in the early days of the twentieth century, with the beginning of management methodology, which a French mining engineer named Henri Fayol conceived. Fayol's strong sense of curiosity and problem-solving became apparent early in his career, demonstrated by his drive to find the right answers to perfectly manage and solve erupting problems, initially within his domain of mining, and eventually across the broader discipline of management.

Following a progressive leadership career in mining and believing that managerial practices were essential to organizational efficiency and predictability, Fayol developed his concept of management, then referred to as "administration." His seminal work, *Administration industrielle et générale*, laid the foundation for modern management theory. Introducing fourteen principles of management, his work had a profound impact on management practices and was referenced widely by others in the field. His ideas became known as Fayolism, and within the framework of Fayol's five primary functions, planning was at the top of the list.

By the late 1950s, there was growing sentiment that the world seemed more predictable, leading to a prevalent belief that the future could be planned. Management by objectives (MBO) became a prevailing current that swept across companies with the promise that if it could be planned, it would happen. This strong MBO surge across businesses globally swelled into "strategic planning." Latching onto this newer concept, internal corporate groups were birthed with the mandate of "planning the future."

Strategic planning is alive and well, though its purpose and promise have evolved from a static planning perspective of "plan it, do it, and it will happen" to a fluid one that accounts for flexibility due to disruption and change. Whether technological advances, global sensitivities, or even a pandemic, we know the future *cannot* be planned with any certainty. Even the best data and the *perfect* plan can ensure little more than possibilities and sometimes probabilities.

A plan must be braided with a tolerance for flexibility. A *perfect* plan is fluid, not fixed. An effective plan is resource-, reality-, risk-, and time-sensitive.

The Perfection Plunge

Fluid planning requires fluid thinking. When thinking is fixed on an ideal, protecting the plan can feel like a way to ensure the ideal future state. However, anchors of idealism and control work against these captains, provoking *perfectionism*—a disabling kink to planning and ideal outcomes.

While "healthy" perfectionism can drive high standards and goal achievement, maladaptive perfectionism can drive *excessively* high standards due to insecurities including fear of failure, criticism, or imperfection, hindering performance.

Captains of Ocean Boiling are prone to what I call the *perfection plunge*. Striving for a plan that will flawlessly control and deliver an ideal outcome deceives these leaders into a mental mesh of perfectionism. Intending to avoid the risk of under-delivering, perfectionism urges over-delivering—often, too late.

Perfectionism thwarts productivity by steering the planning process off course in search of more information that will help avoid risk. Captains of Ocean Boiling, can feel productive as long as they are actively in the depths of data and forecasting *analysis*, plunging further and further away from a plan that can be executed!

Planning will always be imperfect, and as the saying goes, "perfect is the enemy of good." Good planning is focused and fluid. Effective planners make decisions in the present that account for potential risk and disruptions along the way to an uncertain future. Perfection never has and never will solve uncertainty. Perfectionism will, however, amplify a planning bias's negative effects, causing these captains to miss the boat on timely and effective execution.

Planning for Purpose
"A good plan violently executed now is better
than a perfect plan executed next week."
—GENERAL GEORGE PATTON

The General's quote is logical and seems pretty simple in essence, doesn't it?

Well, it turns out, planning is often the enemy of action, and the planning fallacy is absolutely the saboteur of effective execution. It's at the root of good-intentioned plans that, well...*don't go according to plan*. And that's because this bias causes plans to go more off-plan than on-plan.

"Planning is bringing the future into the present so
that you can do something about it now."
—ALAN LAKEIN

However, when a plan is hijacked by the planning fallacy, and tangled in perfectionism, a lack of prioritization, scope creep, and overanalysis, it will inevitably veer off course.

When these captains focus on defining what they already know, and what they know they need to know, they're off to a good start in planning. But it's not necessarily the known risks that twist and tangle these captains. Rather, it's the ambiguity of "*unknown* unknowns," a term coined by Donald Rumsfeld, former US secretary of defense, which will make these captains seasick.

In 2002, during a Defense Department briefing, Rumsfeld stated, "There are known knowns. There are things we know that we know. There are known unknowns. That is to say, there are things that we now know we don't know. But there are also unknown unknowns. There are things we do not know we don't know."

The known risk, the uncertainties, and the unknowns are all ocean-boiling triggers that ultimately delay the execution of a "good plan." A plan can be a powerful tool when it is done well. But it loses its power and its value when it is *overdone*. And when it's risk-focused instead of purpose-focused, it becomes restrictive, inflexible, impractical, and a liability to the business instead of a fluid value-creation tool.

Tim Cook's Early Encounters with the Planning Fallacy Mind Knot

Since becoming CEO of Apple in 2011, Tim Cook has become a strong and steady leader of the most valuable brand in America, and the company's success continues to impress analysts and investors.

But his tenure didn't start that way.

With extensive experience in manufacturing and operations, Cook was formerly the chief operating officer at Apple before stepping up to the helm. This was his domain. And yet his expertise in these areas may have provided him with a false sense of assurance, which got in the way of good planning in his early days as CEO. He believed that the products he was bringing forward would make it to the market in the same seamless way earlier products did when he was the company's COO, with ownership for operations. In fact, his reliance on his previous experience did more to harm than help him as a newly minted CEO.

Cook missed some critical things along the way when it came to expanding the product portfolio, as well as compressing the timing in planning the release of new products. His expertise in the very areas that should have prevented the late release of products actually caused him to miss product-release deadlines, not just in one case, but in many.

When Captain Cook assumed the helm at Apple Inc. in 2011, several of the company's new products, including AirPods earbuds, HomePod speakers, and the Apple Watch, as well as critical accessories for the iPad Pro, all arrived consistently late to market, and out of sync with their planned and announced release dates.

As the long-tenured COO of Apple, Cook was widely recognized for the company's excellent record of on-time product delivery to the market. So what happened?

Unlike Steve Jobs, who held new product announcements until a product was ready for shipment, Cook preferred to publicize new products earlier and based on the product availability plan, instead of waiting until the products were actually available for release. Cook's consistent product release delays created long wait periods between Apple's product announcements and the actual shipping of products.

For instance, this was the case in Cook's combined introduction of the iPhone X, 8, and 8 Plus in September 2017. Cook proceeded with this announcement even though he learned the iPhone X would not be ready to ship until six weeks later than planned, due to production bottlenecks. Knowing the late shipping reality of the iPhone X, Cook explained his decision to announce all three products together regardless, claiming he was "giving customers time to choose the phone they preferred."

The financial impact to the business was a 7.6 percent sales decline in the US market in the third quarter of 2017. Customers held off on iPhone purchases during September and October, awaiting the release of the iPhone X. In an interview with the *Wall Street Journal*, Cook acknowledged the miss on sales and then doubled down, excusing the miss by again saying it was best for customers.

Additional errors in prediction included missing the critical Christmas shopping season for AirPods in 2016. Then the company announced HomePods in June 2017, claiming the product would be ready in December. But the company had to issue an update announcing the release of HomePods would be delayed until 2018, and the actual launch date was February of that year. This was a huge planning blunder and a significant deliverable delay on this long-awaited product.

During the protracted release of HomePods, both Amazon and Google took advantage of this market opening to attract sales from otherwise loyal Apple customers and unveiled rival products—a redesigned Echo from Amazon and the Home Max from Google.

The long lead times between announcements and product releases gave competitors time to react, which, in contrast, was precisely what Jobs intended to prevent in sticking with his short lead time announcements. Creating customer disappointment, as well as the risk of their moving to a competitor product, as Apple experienced, cannot be overlooked. It resulted in both a business and financial impact.

A plan is only a plan. Reality rules. As Cook elevated his career to CEO from COO, he found himself in the new position of having many more areas of oversight. With much more data to "boil," honing meaningful insights related to product availability became less efficient and less accurate, making his expertise less effective. Further, with the increase of products and the consequential complexity this added to the company's operations, questions arose regarding a potential pivot by Cook from Apple's focused product portfolio to a bit too much ocean boiling with diversification, which created technology complexity that caused delays, as well as logistical and manufacturing challenges.

NAVIGATION KNOTS AND TACKS

The Planning Bias

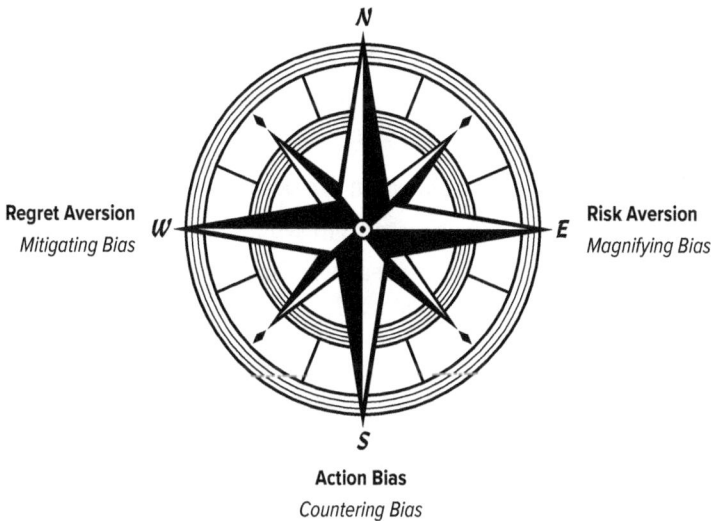

N

Regret Aversion
Mitigating Bias

W

Risk Aversion
Magnifying Bias

E

Action Bias
Countering Bias

S

The Captain's Compass: Captains of Ocean Boiling

North Cardinal Point: The Planning Bias

The planning fallacy bias explains common planning flaws, including overestimating outcomes and underestimating critical factors required to achieve *planned* outcomes, such as missed deadlines, budget overruns, resource restraints, and unaddressed risk. This mind knot also leads to unintended challenges due to perfectionism, flawed prioritization, and ocean boiling sometimes beyond the intended scope of a plan objective.

The consequences of planning fallacy bias are associated with failing to meet planned expectations.

East Cardinal Point: Magnifying Mind Knot

Risk Aversion

Planning is aimed at charting a safe route to a targeted future state. It requires managing uncertainty and identifying and mitigating risk. But the planning fallacy bias causes optimistic distortions, with many unintentional consequences of risk, making these captains risk inducers as well as risk averters. Both their aversion to risk and their unknowing creation of risk can jeopardize their plan.

Risk aversion compels captains to avoid risk. Yet it's their aversion to risk that makes these leaders, Captains of Ocean Boiling, plunge into deep dives of information overload, analysis paralysis, and perfectionism. This unknowingly and unintentionally introduces risk, whether delays or missed deadlines, to their plan due to their propensity to avert risk.

Planning fallacy bias and its optimism undertow also unknowingly create risk with its over- and underestimations. These mind knots, working in collusion, magnify the element of risk in planning.

While Captains of Ocean Boiling seek to mitigate known risks in their plan, they are usually blind to the risk *they create.*

West Cardinal Point: The Mitigating Mind Knot

Regret Aversion

Research shows that regret avoidance is a stronger driver than risk avoidance. Fear of regret potentially resulting from an imperfect plan can be an effective mitigating driver for Captains of Ocean Boiling, making them more attuned to the process of developing the plan.

When regret aversion is in play, it can urge captains toward the option that would seem to cause the least amount of anticipated regret, even if it is not the optimal choice.

Planning involves an unending series of decisions. When regret aversion can command the attention of captains who are prone to overestimating and underestimating important planning factors, this mind knot can help them examine and consider the weight of information and options through a lens of potential regret they may experience for errors in their thinking and planning.

When these leaders intentionally embrace their "regret detector," imagining how a negative outcome would make them feel, they can give themselves the space to think more clearly about their options.

In our earlier example of Tim Cook in his role as CEO of Apple, perhaps adopting a regret aversion mindset could have helped him to narrow the gap between the time he announced new products and when they actually hit the market. Now wouldn't that have spared Cook and Apple a lot of customer disappointment, media criticism, and perhaps personal and professional regret?

South Cardinal Point: The Countering Mind Knot

Action Bias

When Captains of Ocean Boiling struggle to emerge from the sea of information and planning, the Action bias can be the lifeline that pulls them into reality. The serious nature of planning requires the right data, thoughtful analysis, and strong forecasting. The planning process typically requires a measured pace. We've examined how conspiring and compelling forces of risk aversion and perfectionism can cause these captains to "boil the ocean," anchoring them in the planning process, significantly delaying execution of the plan.

The action bias can provide a valuable thrust for these leaders, urging them to move in the direction of execution and action rather than stagnation. Action bias breaks analysis paralysis inertia, enabling early learning and momentum and the opportunity for timely and fluid adjustments.

This bias comes with its own cautionary note. The action mind knot working independently can move a leader to action without the necessary data and evidence to fortify and justify that their activities will actually lead to achieving targeted objectives. Unmanaged, action bias can deceive leaders to mistake activity for productivity when actions are misaligned. The urgency of this mind knot can lead to quick decisions in response to pressure or a desire to appear decisive. And, moving too fast can lead to misallocation of resources, overlooked long-term consequences, or resistance to new information that might suggest a course correction.

Yet, as a counter to planning bias, it can be an antidote to planning paralysis.

NAVIGATING PLANNING FALLACY BIAS

Questions: Know Your Knots

- Do I tend to be overly optimistic about how long things will take in my planning initiatives?
- Have I encountered budget overruns or unexpected costs in past initiatives? Was it because I underestimated expenses?
- Do I tend to overlook potential risks or obstacles when setting goals or making plans for the future?
- Have I underestimated the complexity of projects in the past, leading to delays or difficulties in execution?
- When planning, do I build in contingency plans and buffer time and resources to account for unexpected delays or setbacks?
- Am I effective at collaborating with stakeholders to gather input and to ensure that my planning is based on a comprehensive understanding of the situation.
- Am I willing to adjust my plan and timelines when new information or circumstances warrant it, or do I stay tied to my initial estimates?

Tacking Techniques

- Anchor forecasts and projections based on actual past results and adjust for current realities that can impact the route forward.

- Reference similar planning initiatives of others, including their completion metrics, to inform estimates on timelines and other factors.
- Build buffers into your plan to account for obstacles, delays, and other occurrences that will inevitably occur.
- Break big planning initiatives and projects into components and set implementation intentions for each piece.
- Keep plan objectives, including its scope, front and center to avoid ocean boiling.
- Plan realistically, not perfectly. Engage in deliberate, diligent deep dives that align with defined objectives and targeted outcomes.
- Approach strategies and plans as fluid and not fixed to ensure flexibility.

THE RATIONAL SOLUTION

How Heineken Practiced Agile Planning

In 1864, a young man by the name of Gerard Heineken bought an Amsterdam brewery, De Hooiberg, and immediately turned his focus toward brewing premium lager beer rather than the more typical drinking ales and porters that the Dutch were familiar with at the time. In 1873, he began brewing Bavarian lager, which became the flagship beer of his new brewery. This "gentleman's beer" set Heineken apart from the plentiful commodity of "working-class" beer brands of the time.

Over a century and a half later, Heineken upholds the same premium market positioning, as well as prominence as the beer of choice for sports and craft beer enthusiasts, and even for non-drinkers with its Heineken 0.0, which launched the company to the top of the alcohol-free market.

The company's strategy, planning, and execution approach through the years has resulted in Heineken sustaining its iconic brand as the number two global brewing company behind the massive Anheuser Busch InBev.

So how did the company achieve this across the generations of Heineken leadership?

The answer is solid planning combined with agility. Heineken treated *strategy* and *planning* as verbs instead of nouns. Throughout the years, both planning and strategy were fluid and fortified in multiple ways.

In the early years of the company's evolution, a strong commitment to innovation, both in ingredient formulation and their branding and marketing initiatives, ultimately created the basis for passage forward both domestically and in international markets. Heineken's steady and methodical planning was the key to global success. The company followed key planning principles, including keeping their focus on clear objectives, while remaining flexible.

Heineken's foray into international geographic markets was possible because of cooperative planning throughout the organization, along with a strong bias for action. The principle of cooperative planning was evident in the Heineken culture as far back as 1932 when Heineken's export manager, on a trip to Singapore, encouraged a Scottish producer of lemonade to expand into beer production. Partnering with the businessman, Malayan Breweries

Limited was formed. Tiger Beer became its flagship product, and ultimately, Asia's best-selling beer.

Strategically, Heineken then introduced beer into countries that had no locally produced beer nor the means to produce it. Heineken's plan and sensitivity to timing in investing in local brands also successfully grew domestic demand for locally brewed beer. In addition, the company recognized the opportunity to import its other brands into international markets, subsequently increasing demand for options beyond locally brewed products.

Competitive planning, strategy, and a bias for action enabled Heineken to dominate these markets and countries without delay and at a rapid pace. The surgical focus of the plan also provided the company with an efficient, tested, and proven map to advance its international mission, acquiring even larger markets. The combination of strategic planning and practical and tactical execution led to the company's international expansion and became the DNA of Heineken.

When the founder's young grandson joined the business in 1941, his marketing talent was evident, and he too focused on plans for innovation and growth that were swiftly tested and executed. Freddy Heineken understood the principle of planning for the future, and he focused on getting to the future state of the company through "brand promise." He successfully introduced the patented "smiling e" in the iconic Heineken logo, along with the five-point red star, long used by brewers to signify the five ingredients of beer including barley, water, hops, yeast, and the "magic of brewing." These two planned and timely executed marketing and branding moves strengthened Heineken's globally recognized brand name and its association with quality beer.

The Planning Principle of Cooperation and Partnership
Heineken is the successful global brand and business it is today because of leveraging planning principles, along with a bias for action, the combination of which mitigated the perils of the planning fallacy. The company was focused and never lost sight of its sustained commitment to planning *and* moving ahead.

Heineken has excelled in blending fortified and agile planning with disciplined action and appropriate timing, enabling the company to forereach, achieving its goals in both local and global markets. From a market penetration and global presence standpoint, the company's strategy was all about the right timing, engaging the right partners, and targeting the right communities. With the precision of research and timing, Heineken planned their entry into markets at the right time, enabling the company to create a committed local network while establishing the Heineken brand as the market leader.

A strong plan of action, focused decisions, purposeful processes, and the right timing has accounted for Heineken's overall success. In addition to innovation, which launched the brand, disciplined action or processes built to support the company's objectives cannot be overlooked. For instance, when Heineken recognized a decline in alcohol consumption around the globe due to a growing awareness of the harmful effects of alcohol, the company saw the opportunity to take a market leadership role in the non-alcoholic beer market. Through an investment in research, the company created a non-alcoholic product that nearly replicated the taste of a regular Heineken beer — Heineken 0.0—moving the company to the top of the non-alcoholic market.

In the craft beer space, Heineken also made its mark. The company recognized that not only their name, but also their story, would be their winning strategy. So, to win in this market, Heineken used a "reverse marketing approach." Rather than rely on their sponsorship of large events, the company agilely rolled their craft beer out via tasting experiences and small events. Beerwulf, a Heineken brand, was created as its own entity. Growing from 400 weekly orders to 400 orders per hour in a year's time, Heineken's craft beer strategy and course of action proved to be a winning approach.

Planning and Action – Ready, Set, Go

Simply having an awareness of these pervasive mental tangles is not enough to prevent the flawed thinking and suboptimal decisions and behaviors they cause. The planning fallacy bias is no different.

Planning, whether strategic, operational, tactical, or contingency, demands clear thinking, good analysis, and unbiased judgment and decision-making to mitigate errors and risk, and to achieve future state predictions. While predicting aims to reduce uncertainty about the future, planning aims to prepare for it. Yet, the planning fallacy bias gets in the way of effective planning and good outcomes.

However, when the planning fallacy bias is aided by the *action bias*, predictions and outcomes can look quite different.

We've seen how planning can easily go off course due to planning fallacy bias because of its optimistic inclination and navigational hazards that can paralyze planning effectiveness. Yet, an agile counter-bias strategy can ensure fortified plans fluidly move from excessive planning to execution.

Strategically adopting value drivers associated with action bias can help to keep captains on track with planning and focus while inspiring urgency and avoiding disruptions, such as perfectionistic spiraling and other residual pitfalls of the planning bias.

In other words, while overplanning can tie leaders in place, delaying action, the action mind knot urges movement.

On its own, action bias moves us to action, with or without good reason. Yet in combination with value drivers of principled planning, these two mind knots can empower plan fortification and acceleration for timely execution.

So, I've given this concept a name: the Fortified Forereaching Model. This model harnesses the upside of both planning and action and offers Captains of Ocean Boiling the framework to *forereach*, moving forward from planning to execution, and toward outcomes that are achieved on time, on budget, and on point.

The Fortified Forereaching Model:
The Rational Way Forward

Forereaching is a nautical term used in sailing that basically means moving ahead or maintaining headway while forging into the wind. Forereaching is a tacking technique to ensure forward motion and progress despite strong headwinds. And sometimes, it can even enable captains to forge ahead, accelerating their journey and surpassing other boats that may be on a parallel mission.

Captains of Ocean Boiling can be powerful leaders because of their natural ability to protect their organizations from risk while planning a safe course to an uncertain future. When these leaders act with timeliness, either because they carry a natural action bias along with their planning fallacy mind knot, or because they create rules or strategies to move effectively from planning to execution, they are in a better position to bolster rather than bind their performance and that of their company.

Like a cleat hitch knot that keeps a boat tied to a dock, excessive planning keeps these captains and their boats safely secured to the dock instead of sailing toward the planned horizon.

The Fortified Forereaching model provides a rational way forward for risk-averse and slow-to-act captains who get bogged down in crafting the perfect plan, causing them to remain docked in the planning harbor.

The spirit of planning is precaution, purpose, and positive outcomes. Planning, you might say, is a fortification mission for Captains of Ocean Boiling who are naturally inclined to develop strong and effective plans.

The critical differentiator for these captains is knowing when to transition from planning to action. When these leaders leverage the precision of their knowledge to not only forecast and plan strategically, but to effectively transition their "fortified" predictions into action through a timely, practical, and deliberate operating plan, they can set themselves apart.

THE BOTTOM LINE: ALL HANDS ON DECK

The strategies below are intended to serve as potential guardrails to help organizations better navigate the pitfalls of the planning fallacy bias, while leveraging the benefits of the action bias.

The Fortified Forereaching model ties planning and action together. It helps guide behaviors across the organization with an approach that blends thoughtful planning, swift action, continuous feedback, and flexibility in planning and project execution—promoting plans that are realistic and move forward toward targeted outcomes.

The Fortified Forereaching Mission Objectives

- Harness the power and principles of planning with the appropriate urgency and action to enable forereaching outcomes.
- Guard against scope creep, analysis paralysis, and the "perfection plunge," which lead to unfocused planning and compromised plan execution, including missed timelines, budget overages, resource oversights, and ultimately suboptimal outcomes.

The Strategy Equation

Planning Fallacy Bias + Action Bias =
The Fortified Forereaching Model

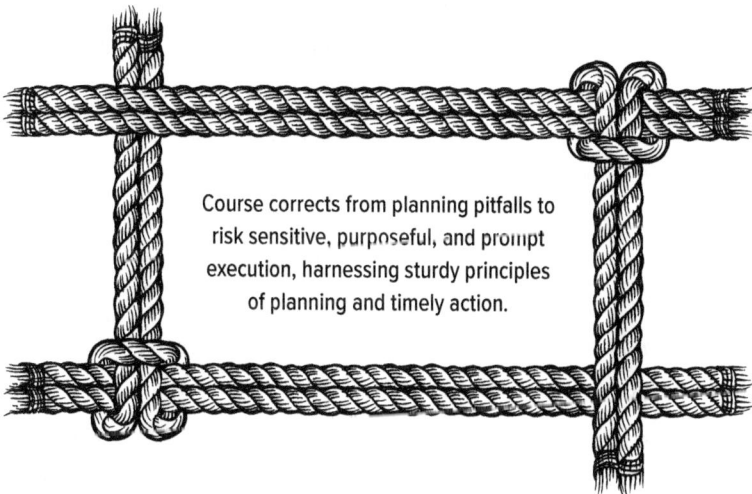

Course corrects from planning pitfalls to risk sensitive, purposeful, and prompt execution, harnessing sturdy principles of planning and timely action.

Strategic Maneuvers and Organizational Guidance: The Fortified Forereaching Model

The Captain

- Institute agile planning practices that consider top-down ideas as well as bottom-up realities, enabling flexibility, dynamic course changes, and timely action.
- Leverage the inherent optimism of the planning fallacy bias to inspire the team, setting ambitious goals. Simultaneously employ the action bias to initiate early, test assumptions, and make adjustments in real time.
- Implement time-bound planning sessions to prevent overplanning, encouraging movement from planning to execution.
- Identify the most critical objectives for the initiative and prioritize them.
- Consider best-case and worst-case scenarios when planning to increase awareness of potential outcomes and preparation for uncertainties.
- Establish a cadence for review meetings and feedback cycles with key stakeholders to evaluate assumptions against results, allowing for timely course correction where assumptions prove to be flawed.
- Assign a team to intentionally find flaws and limitations to the proposed plan to challenge assumptions and to identify potential pitfalls.
- Avoid anchoring to an *ideal* plan. If new information suggests a shift, adjust the sails.
- Assume optimism will kink the plan, obfuscating threats and risk. Develop a checklist of potential plan perils,

to account for risk and the ways in which optimism can skew projections, pushing the plan outside of its channel markers.

The Crew—Leadership Team

- Tie each functional sub-plan to the overall organizational plan with clarity of purpose to avoid activities that will veer off course.
- Document goals and plans in writing to keep everyone on the same page regarding scope and timeline, to reduce misunderstanding, mistakes, miscommunication, and missed targets.
- Add buffers to plan estimates to ensure deadlines can be met, even if there is an unexpected delay or problem.
- Reference similar situations and plans before estimating time and cost, for a more realistic basis for predictions and greater odds for achieving targeted outcomes.
- Identify "action" accountability partners at the business segment or functional level to help counter perfection plunges that would delay timely forward movement, tying down execution.
- Break larger plans into smaller milestones with clear deadlines. Take a granular approach to estimating by breaking activities into smaller tasks with specific deadlines and financial targets, forcing planning that avoids larger generalized assumptions.
- Champion contingency operating plans that are updated regularly and can swiftly be mobilized in the event the original plan fails.

People Processes

- Select leaders with proven planning skills and with a track record of appropriate timeliness in planning and execution.
- Develop an enterprise-wide management program designed to increase awareness of planning pitfalls and the value of purposeful swift action. Include preemptive strategies to counteract errors in timing and resource planning.
- Design and implement compensation incentive plans that drive and reward thoughtful and timely planning and execution.
- Foster a culture that recognizes the pitfalls of planning fallacy bias and values the benefit of timely action and adaptability.

Financial Considerations

- Track the ROI of *time-based* deliverables, highlighting risk and the diminishing returns associated with missed deadlines.
- Provide financial modeling and predictive analytics to minimize risk, and to illustrate potential financial outcomes of plans. Illustrate how certain changes will impact the plan, allowing for adjustments while avoiding costly missteps due to a lack of foresight.
- Support the organization with decision tools that enable multiple scenarios to be explored, including the potential consequences of each option.
- Provide real-time expense tracking for plans, allowing for immediate course correction where actual expenses deviate from projections.

Commercial Considerations

- Adopt dynamic forecasting to adjust sales forecasts regularly, based on real-time data.
- Structure a feedback loop to avoid communication breakdowns resulting in delays and missed deadlines due to overly optimistic timelines in customer agreements or deliverables.
- Include buffer time when forecasting the conversion of prospects into customers, allowing for unexpected circumstances or delays.
- Implement time- and action-based sales plans, encouraging steady and timely movement through each stage of the sales process to create momentum, while steadily forereaching in the market.
- Adjust plans on the go. Foster a culture of market agility by prioritizing quick responses to changing market dynamics and emerging opportunities.
- Review plans where timelines may have been underestimated, and take corrective action accordingly. Adjust and fortify the plan to ensure it provides the necessary forereaching capabilities for competitive advantage.

Board Considerations

- Schedule frequent strategy reviews to ensure long-term plans continue to align with market realities and organizational capabilities.
- Implement a practice of review and iteration of major plans, planning in shorter, iterative bursts, enabling

reflection on progress and challenges, and replanning the next phase based on real-world data for both foresight and adaptability.

· Require a clear timeline for milestone achievements, tracking at each stage of the plan to understand where progress is lagging.

· Ensure the organization has an established risk management framework in place and an action-oriented approach to swiftly address risk associated with overly optimistic planning.

Five Questions to Identify Indicators of Planning Fallacy Bias

1. Can you recall an initiative you've planned and led that didn't go according to plan? How well did your initial time and resources estimates compare to actual outcomes?

2. How frequently do you consult with your team or external stakeholders when making project estimates or setting timelines?

3. Do you tend to stick with overly optimistic estimates, even in the face of evidence that suggests otherwise?

4. Has there been an instance where you had to modify your plan significantly midway through a project? How did you navigate through the change?

5. When faced with uncertainty in an initiative, how do you factor that into your planning and decision-making process?

TAKEAWAYS: TYING IT TOGETHER

Captains of Ocean Boiling

Captains of Ocean Boiling are risk-averse, planning-oriented leaders, who can "Boil the Ocean" in search of information and ways to mitigate risk, attempting to develop and achieve the future for which they are planning.

These captains fear failure, and planning offers a perceived assurance of control, allowing them to optimistically believe their plan will lead to the future state they imagine. Sometimes "perfection plungers," Captains of Ocean Boiling will miscalculate headwinds of time, resources, and challenges, resulting in a "perfectly imperfect" plan delaying execution and deliverables.

Predisposed to the planning fallacy bias, these planners are optimistically swayed toward underestimating critical plan factors and overestimating outcome expectations. Though well intentioned to avert risk, these leaders can unknowingly induce risk, finding themselves adrift in excessive data and analysis, losing sight of their horizon, setting their plan off course, and compromising the window for effective course correction.

Planning Fallacy Bias

The planning fallacy bias explains why planning doesn't usually go according to plan. This mind knot is responsible for the many kinks in the phenomenon of prediction. This bias affects future outcomes by causing captains to miss out on their predictions, whether deadlines, resources, budgets, challenges, or even opportunities, posing a significant threat to the realization of their *ideal* plans.

Whether plans are too controlling, inflexible, or out of sync with realities of timing, resources and challenges, captains affected by the planning fallacy bias leave others in the wake of their plans to follow and comply, and often with no option to adjust. Prominent issues associated with this mind knot include underestimating timing, resources, budget, and hurdles, along with overestimating outcomes.

The Rational Solution: The Fortified Forereaching Model

This model is a rational navigational framework for Captains of Ocean Boiling, combining the power of disciplined planning principles, the optimistic undercurrent of the planning fallacy bias, and the forward movement of action bias for captains and organizations to make headway from planning to timely execution.

The framework offers a forward-moving approach to fortified planning, risk mitigation, and the execution momentum required to achieve objectives on time, on budget, and on plan.

CONCLUSION

We have met the enemy, and the enemy is us.
—COMMODORE OLIVER HAZARD PERRY

Cognitive and emotional biases are a human condition—no one is immune. As I've attempted to point out in my writing, biases are at play whether you realize it or not. Deeply entrenched in our human psyche, they shape our perceptions, weaving a narrative in our minds, swaying our thinking and emotions, and often misguiding our judgment, the decisions we make, and the actions we take.

Biases can be quite useful in situations that demand a quick reaction to an immediate circumstance. But when it comes to leadership and its complexities, mind knots can more often work against your best interests, prioritizing impulse over intention, the moment over the mission, and the self over service to the people, organizations, and strategic initiatives you lead. Mind knots warrant your awareness and attention.

As we've seen through the many stories throughout the book, left unchecked, mind knots do and will hijack rational leadership.

The problem is, we are usually blind to our unconscious forces. Learning about biases can help us to spot them in ourselves and in others, which is often easier to do.

Our mind is the lens through which we view everything. If we choose to bury our heads in the sand, a bias known as the ostrich effect, we put ourselves in a vulnerable position, deferring to our biases, with no strategy to manage them in situations when we most need to do so. Understanding mind knots will help you avoid the self-defeating consequences they will too often cause in swaying your thinking and behaviors in compromising ways.

By getting out of your own way, so to speak, and by taking the lead rather than being led by these forces that *direct* you without your permission, and often without your even knowing, you will be better positioned in your leadership and your life.

You cannot eliminate mind knots. However, the misperceptions and misdirection a mind knot causes can be avoided with intentional intervention through practices and processes that combine a mind knot with another countervailing mind knot. The pairing of the two biases yields what is called "the rational solution." This is not about eradicating biases. It's about harnessing their strengths in synchrony, with each mind knot improving the performance of the other for a combined outcome that neither bias could produce on its own.

This strategy underscores a critical insight—since you can't beat them, you can join them. Intentionally leveraging the competitive tension, the push and pull of each bias, you can achieve a more rational approach to judgment and decisions, allowing your mind knots to work for instead of against you and your organization.

OUR MIND KNOTS JOURNEY

As we navigated through the book, we explored eight primary biases, each of which presents intrinsic entanglements to leadership in a unique way. Armed with an understanding of these mind knots, their cognitive and emotional currents, and usual negative consequences, we found our way to "the rational solution"—a counter-bias or *double knot* strategy.

We saw there are two ways to get to a rational solution. The first approach is *agile thinking*, which is difficult to do and harder to sustain given the force of biases, yet effective in certain situations. The Captain's Compass addresses the directionality of these mind knots, showing how conspiring biases can affect the intensity of a prominent bias by either magnifying, mitigating, or countering its effects. Its purpose is to help you understand conspiring biases that will increase risk, and biases that can work in cooperation with one or more of your prominent biases to better position you for less risk and greater odds of success. The compass is intended to provide short-term techniques at the individual level.

The larger issue is that over time, patterns of decision-making and behavior can become apparent across an organization, often due to a leader's prominent bias, which creates signals, swaying decisions and actions across the enterprise. As the leader goes, so goes the organization.

To address the pervasiveness of mind knots, each chapter proposes a second approach—an organizational intervention in the form of a model that protects the organization from the potential risk associated with the prominent mind knot featured in the chapter. Based on a paradoxical approach, each model empowers and harnesses the positive attributes of the main bias and outlines countermeasures to manage the bias from the helm to the realm. The primary mission of each model is to provide an actionable intervention strategy with agile methodologies and practices, providing guardrails and protection for the leader and the organization by promoting flexibility, feedback, perspectives, collaboration, integration, process, and prioritization. This sets the course for a value-driven approach to decision-making and action-taking—*an uninviting environment for mind knots.*

This paradoxical or bias-countering strategy offers an effective intervention to the detrimental influence of mind knots in leadership and more broadly in life.

We began our journey with the Egocentric bias and its self-centric pull, amplifying self-importance and personal perspective, while sidelining valuable perspectives of others. We saw how Overconfidence bias can magnify ego effects, and how Positive Outcome bias, often conspiring with egocentrism, results in a blind focus on an intended positive outcome often at the expense of a sound journey. The rational solution, referred to as the Egonomic Enrichment Model, leverages the selflessness of Altruism bias to counter the selfishness of ego.

The Curse of Knowledge bias silently casts a blinding effect on leaders and domain experts, preventing them from seeing a clear path to transferring their knowledge in a way that can be understood by those who are less *knowing*. This mind knot can create significant communication barriers, resulting in tangled and frayed messaging and misaligned expectations. It can prevent a leader's knowledge from becoming a source of value and power to the organization. Leveraging Picture Superiority effect as a counter-strategy to this knowledge knot enables a rational solution for streamlining complex knowledge into simple, consumable messaging, transforming knowledge into actionable power. This is accomplished with the Inconspicuous Influencer Model.

In Chapter 4, we explored the Illusion of Control bias and its tendency to deceive leaders into believing they have more control over events than is actually the case. Their sense of control is usually intensified by Illusory Superiority, leading to disillusionment. These commanding coils often create micromanagement and other counterproductive issues, tying these leaders and their organizations down. The agility of the Framing Effect combined with the rigid controlling illusion of this mind knot can transform command-and-control leaders into empowering leaders who inspire through the rational route outlined in the Insistent Inspirer Model.

Conformity bias and its conspiring cousin, Groupthink, insidiously taint and tie all hands and minds together, compelling them to act in accordance with the group. They too often steer in a direction that is not in the best interest of key business objectives or the organization. However, due to many factors, and sometimes prevailing symbolic norms, such as a *consensus* culture, poor decisions are made because of conforming factors, diverting from the business's salient objectives. Outcome bias, different from Positive Outcome bias we saw in Chapter 2, used as a countering force to the misdirection of conformity bias can keep leaders and decision-makers steering toward business objectives. The Inclusive Outcome Model lays out a rational route, charting a new course to protect consensus-driven captains and organizations from the often negative effects of Conformity and Groupthink in decision-making.

While a positive outlook can be a tremendous asset to a leader and to the organization, excessive optimism, or the Optimism bias, can have a negative effect. Optimism bias can blindside leaders, causing them to overlook risks, leaving them unprepared in their sail for headwinds they may face. Combining the countering, "glass half empty" mindset urged by Pessimism bias with the positive outlook of optimism provides a rational way forward for these dream-pursuing captains. The suggested practices outlined in the Dream "Ketcher" Model shift the sails from unrestrained optimism to rational optimism, empowering the realistic achievement of dreams and outcomes for the captain and the organization.

Belief bias can cause tunnel vision, limiting a leader's perspective and keeping them committed to the conclusion or outcome they believe. Often lacking discernment and turning a blind eye toward risk, this mind knot keeps leaders showboating, compromising their adaptability and their ability to course-correct when they should. Regret aversion can provide an effective countering effect to these believers, causing them to anticipate the regret they will feel should their belief prove instead to bind them to a losing outcome. The Enduring Enchanter Model charts a course to restage blind belief into evidence-based belief, increasing the probability of enduring outcomes.

Intuition bias, like optimism, can be a leader's gift. Yet, originating in a personal repository of experience, this mind knot can also lead to inaccurate perceptions and decisions made without logical reasoning. The strong emotional undercurrent of intuition often causes these gifted leaders to bypass critical data and the analysis necessary for informed navigation, shifting their gift into their gnarl. Countering intuition with the Logic bias steadies the ship, empowering intuition with thoughtful, logical reasoning. The Sound and Savvy Model provides the navigation map to a rational way forward for intuitively intelligent captains.

Planning Fallacy bias, also riding the wave of optimism, causes overestimations in outcomes and underestimations in time, costs, and risks associated with an initiative, leaving a leader unprepared for unexpected realities in execution and leading to unmet expectations. These leaders, tasked with preparing for risk, can also become perfection plungers, leading to further delays and risk. The counter strategy for the risk-induced pitfalls of over-planning is to leverage the pragmatism of the Action bias. This strategy course corrects from planning pitfalls to risk-sensitive, purposeful, and prompt execution, harnessing the sturdy principles of planning and timely action. The rational approach outlined in the Fortified Forereaching Model can help these captains to make headway from planning to execution, with an appropriately timed and fortified plan.

TYING IT TOGETHER AND PUTTING MIND KNOTS TO GOOD USE

"Much is known about the conditions under which each
bias is likely to influence judgments and decisions, and
a fair amount is known that would allow an observer of
decision-making to recognize biased thinking in real time."
—DANIEL KAHNEMAN

We must remember, biases are directional, swaying us toward or away from a tendency. Therefore, the burden is on us to develop an awareness of their pushes and pulls, so we can take the lead rather than be unknowingly led.

To improve our judgment and decision-making, we would be wise to know and understand potential enemies within ourselves—our mind knots. We won't always be aware of when our mind knots are positioned to prevail in any given circumstance. Yet our decisions, behaviors, and emotions, prompted by our unconscious inclinations, can change the course of our leadership, possibly directing a course that cannot be reversed.

Mind Knots provides the opportunity to increase your awareness and understanding about psychological bias and how biases impact how and why you make the choices you make. Paying attention to patterns in your decision processes, choices, emotions, and actions will provide you with clues about your potential biases.

You can use the tools and bias intervention strategies throughout the book, adapting them to develop your own approach to managing your biases. And ideally, you can expand these intervention strategies to better manage cognitive and emotional biases that may be impacting leadership across your organization.

Understanding and recognizing your biases has practical value in the day-to-day of your leadership, including when you are choosing leaders for your organization, because bias is a hidden cost to your bottom line.

FINAL COMMENTS

I don't have all the answers, but I do know that to achieve the best solutions, you need to ask the right questions.

Questions are our power tools, inspiring a pause in our thinking and potentially shifting our perspective to improve our judgment, *consciously* swaying us in a thoughtful manner.

Asking the right questions enables us to look beyond symptoms, and instead to the unconscious obstacle that is often at the root of the issues with which we grapple—mind knots. Use this book and the questions provided in each chapter as a reminder to check yourself, your team, and groups across your organization for evidence of cognitive and emotional biases that may hinder your mission.

Before we end this voyage, I will remind you of the simple yet powerful overarching question I suggested you ask yourself in the book's introduction: *Who am I practicing becoming?*

Ask yourself this question every day. Because what you practice is what matters. Practice identifying and recognizing your cognitive and emotional biases. Then practice managing them. Let this question be your guide and filter, *consciously* directing you, rather than ceding control to your unconscious tendencies, which will otherwise lead the way.

Know your knots—the knots that tie you in place, and the knots that can give you speed and move you forward.

Thank you for joining me on this voyage!

Continuing Your Mind Knots Journey

There's a lot to absorb and unpack in this book. You can continue your *Mind Knots* journey at *mindknots.co*. Here you will find multiple resources for a deeper dive into the forty-plus psychological biases referenced throughout the chapters, as well as others that simply could not be addressed within the limitations of the book.

I developed *mindknots.co* as a resource to continue the work of this book—to heighten awareness of the cognitive limitations and challenges psychological biases present in leadership. On the site, you will find a comprehensive index of mind knots, including those in the book and beyond. Additional resources include bias checklists, suggested interview questions to identify specific biases, and best practice frameworks and debiasing strategies for a sound decision-making process. These resources, tools, and strategies are intended to better position you and your team to recognize and manage the mind knots that may be impacting leadership across your organization.

Bon voyage for now! Wishing you successful navigation in your leadership journey.

ACKNOWLEDGEMENTS

The two people who really made this book possible are my sons, Michael, and Cody, from whom I learn every day. Thank you both for your unwavering encouragement and enthusiasm over the past four-plus years, and for tolerating the many nights and weekends of writing, editing, more writing, and unavoidably hearing a computer-generated voice read the words I had written back to me repeatedly, chapter by chapter, until I was satisfied with my writing and message. Thank you for enduring all of it—and continually cheering me on! Thank you for genuinely being true to who you both are every day—it drives me more than you can know in my purpose and my work.

I will be forever grateful to the amazing leaders (both clients and candidates) with whom I've had the pleasure and privilege to work with and learn from. Thank you to the many business and thought partners across my leadership network, many of whom encouraged me to extend my voice and perspective more broadly, and all of whom contributed unique and valuable insights along the course of my career and my *Mind Knots* journey. Among these are Suzanne

Kennard of One of One Coaching, Peggy Wagner of Optimizing Talent, and Mary Steiber Reynhout of Navigate Forward.

A very warm thank you to Dr. E. Ted Prince for writing the foreword for *Mind Knots*, and most importantly for encouraging and inspiring me through the early stages of the book. Your work and wisdom has inspired me since we first became acquainted, adding meaning to my work and throughout this book journey. Many thanks for your suggestion to incorporate the concept of a compass, which became the Captain's Compass in keeping with the theme of the book.

I am very grateful to Sheri Thillman, who continues to deliver value and support—managing so many things related to my business, especially during the time-sensitive final stages of writing and publishing.

A heartfelt thank you to all my early readers: friends, colleagues, leaders in my community, and clients who took the time to read through chapters of the book, especially through some rough and unpolished patches, to provide valuable feedback, and thank you to all of you who graciously offered a comment for the book. The perspective I gained through your diverse lenses helped me to understand how my message was being received, informing my final manuscript tweaks. A special thanks to Hal Reiter, Mike McCann, Cary Broussard, Law Burks, Rose Bentley, Bill Haldane, Aric Olson, Fran Luisi, Stephan Newhouse, and Jeff Graby.

Many thanks also to my amazing and supportive friends, including Carin and Richard Dupuis, Morgan and Julie McKeown, Mark and Gina Esposito, and Doug Stevens, each of whom offered candid feedback and perspective through the combined lenses of executive search, coaching, business leadership and growth, private equity, and financial services.

Thank you to the experts in the field of leadership, business, and psychology, whose influence, inspiration, concepts, and insights have taught me much. Special thanks to the pioneers and masters in behavioral science, many of whom I have quoted in the book, for their wisdom, extensive research, studies, and published work that continues to inform and broaden my thinking and perspective of psychological bias. Among those who have indirectly influenced and impacted my perspective are Daniel Kahneman, (whose 400-plus page books I enthusiastically devour), Richard Thaler, Olivier Sibony, Cass Sunstein, Dan Ariely, Malcolm Gladwell, Ryan Holiday, Shane Parrish, David Epstein, Brad Stulberg, Steve Magness, John C. Maxwell, Marshall Goldsmith, Daniel Goleman, Ram Charan, Max Bazerman, Dan Moore, Dan Sullivan, and Dr. Benjamin Hardy.

Finally, I could not have brought this book forward without the exceptional expertise of the team with whom I worked to make *Mind Knots* a reality. A heartfelt thank you to my extraordinary editor, Tom Lane, who conscientiously and expertly guided me through structural and line edits, teaching me valuable lessons that improved my writing along the way.

Thank you to Anna Dorfman for capturing the essence of *Mind Knots* through a book cover design that says it all.

A big thank you to Adam Coffey, author of *Empire Builder*, *The Private Equity Playbook*, and *The Exit Strategy Playbook*, who graciously introduced me to the incredible team who supported me throughout the publishing process, led by Kristin Clark of Elite Content Creation, LLC. This could not have all come together without Kristin's expertise in managing the many intricacies of the publishing process in order to turn *Mind Knots* from my manuscript into this book, which can now carry my voice and message far beyond the span I could have reached on my own.

Kristin, thank you for your expertise and for working side by side with me, managing the details of the publishing process, and tying all the technical pieces together through a well-executed plan that resulted in a terrific outcome.

To John van der Woude, JDVW Designs, who masterfully transformed my imperfect graphic renderings into simple and clear graphics that appear throughout the book, and who masterfully engineered its interior layout with a special eye toward readability, a tremendous thank you.

And a big thank you to Kelly Teemer of Teems PR, LLC, whose marketing, PR savvy, and diligent guidance helped introduce and create visibility for *Mind Knots* among leadership and business audiences that could benefit from its message.

ABOUT THE AUTHOR

Lisa Tromba is Managing Partner and Founder of Lisa Tromba Associates, an executive search and leadership solutions firm (formerly Luisi Tromba Advisors, of which she was Co-Founder and Managing Partner). Lisa also leads Leadership Intelligence Services, LLC, which she founded in 2010 to support her clients and her business with executive assessment capabilities.

She currently partners with clients across Private Equity and privately held mid-market organizations, where she is recognized for her high-touch/high-impact approach to executive search and broader leadership solutions. For more than 25 years, she has guided organizations from mid-market enterprises to Fortune 50 companies in searching for and selecting executive leaders.

Previously a partner in three global executive search firms, including Odgers Berndtson and A.T. Kearney, then an EDS company, she held earlier roles in search including with Herbert Mines Associates, a prominent retail/consumer search firm. Lisa's executive search career was launched after several years within a

Private Equity environment, and her early business experience was developed during her foundational years with IBM.

Lisa publishes *LeaderEdge*, an email newsletter sharing timeless and timely insights, provocative ideas, and frameworks inspired by prominent thought leaders, which her leadership community can use to sharpen their leadership edge. Lisa is referenced in the book, *From Cinderella to CEO*, and her articles have been published in *Chief Executive Magazine* and *American Management Association*, among other business publications.

Lisa holds a Master's degree in Communications from Fairfield University, and she is credentialed in multiple leadership assessment tools and approaches.

She lives in Stamford, CT with her two sons, Michael and Cody. You can connect with Lisa at *ltaexecsearch.com* and *leadership intell.com*. Subscribe to LeaderEdge at *leaderedge.leaderlens.io*.

www.ingramcontent.com/pod-product-compliance
Lightning Source LLC
Chambersburg PA
CBHW062116020426
42335CB00013B/991